TOXIC MOTHERS

Finding Virtue, Integrity, and Love
One Rule at a Time

Cover Design by Melissa Williams Design

Editing by Rachel Shuster

Interior Graphics by COR Design

Interior Formatting by Melissa Williams Design

ISBN: 978-1-958364-00-0 Paperback Edition
ISBN: 978-1-958364-01-7 eBook Edition

HELP YOURSELF
PUBLISHING COMPANY, LLC
Helping You Write All Along Your Journey

Visit www.guyarcuri.com

TOXIC MOTHERS

Finding Virtue, Integrity, and Love
One Rule at a Time

A Son's Guide to Healing
and Moving On

GUY ARCURI

DISCLAIMERS

Disclaimer: The author is not a licensed professional and does not engage in rendering professional medical, psychological, or psychiatric advice. There is no substitute for psychotherapy, support groups, or any other form of clinical and professional help. This book can be used as a tool to accompany any kind of medical or psychological advice from licensed and trained physicians, clinicians, therapists, social workers, or clergy. The ideas, references, procedures, and suggestions contained in this book are not intended as a substitute for consulting with your physician. Neither the author nor the publisher nor any resource referenced or cited shall be liable or responsible for any loss or damage allegedly arising from any information or suggestion in this book.

If you or someone you know is experiencing an emotional, mental, or health crisis, please call 911.

Disclaimer: While this book discusses the toxic nature of some of my mother's behaviors, I understand that all humans are complex and multi-faceted beings. No one is 100 percent toxic. As such, I acknowledge that she exhibited loving and tender moments throughout my life, many of which I recall with endearment and gratitude. In addition, I acknowledge that toxic behavior requires permission on some conscious or unconscious level to affect its victim negatively or even positively. That permission is completely my responsibility, no one else's, as are the nature of the recollections of the details in my personal stories. To the best of my ability, I have attempted to represent stories and details of people mentioned in this book but acknowledge that others may have different perspectives.

This is not a book about blame but about taking personal responsibility for healing oneself. None of the illustrations has ill intent to discredit or humiliate my mother posthumously or anyone for that matter. She was a child of God I grew to love maturely as I took charge of my own healing in my adult life. As the author, I have done my very best to re-create events and locations as accurately as possible, but, knowingly, I have changed some names and circumstances to protect the living and the innocent.

FOREWORD

Guy Arcuri and I have known each other for over three decades. We've shared a lot of life together. Along with our wives, we've experienced vacations and holidays, births and deaths, good times and hard times. Though we were in different programs, we got our PhDs on the same day at the same university. His last name was first in the alphabet while my name was at the end, but instead of going up early to hear his name called out at UNC's Kenan Stadium, he hung back with me so we could walk across the stage back-to-back, which made the moment even more special.

That experience is a picture of Guy Arcuri: he puts others ahead of himself and he finds ways to elevate the moment. When we are all together, he is the one who does what others don't want to do, whether it is taking the kids out on adventures when we were all exhausted, doing the dishes after a big meal, running the inconvenient errand, or a thousand other things. He serves others instinctively and joyfully.

His book, *Toxic Mothers*, is a manifestation of his need to serve. Though borne out of some genuine pain, the heart of his book is a deep desire to help men raised by critical, shaming, and manipulative mothers. These wounded women crash boundaries and control their sons, often well into adulthood. Some of these moms are passive-aggressive, some are overtly hostile, and others are neglectful and invalidating. Whatever form it takes, the impact can be devastating on boys and men, leading to years—even decades—of low self-esteem, constant striving, self-medicating, or other unhealthy patterns.

Guy brings his honest, vulnerable style and unique insights to this practical book, sharing his own experiences of living in "Hazel World" and the struggles this produced. While Guy is an accomplished educator, mentor, consultant, and coach, the strength of his book comes from his own lived-in experiences and his accumulated wisdom.

While many guys are blessed with healthy, nurturing mothers, many others are not. As a psychologist in practice for thirty years, my specialty has been therapy with young men. I see the impact of harmful mothers on boys and men on a weekly basis. Having a good resource for them to turn to is invaluable. *Toxic Mothers* takes the reader through three experiences: understanding what has happened, understanding the healing process, and then moving into personal healing. Guy's desire to provide practical strategies to help men become emotionally healthy shines through in this book. There are exercises and reflections designed to bring insight and work through old wounds.

I've known Guy as a person of high integrity and tremendous honesty, a man with a passion for life, a good husband and father, a wise mentor, and a selfless servant of others. He infuses all of these amazing personal qualities into this new book. He pours himself into these words to help bring insight and healing to men who need it.

Dave Verhaagen, PhD
Psychologist and author
Nashville, Tennessee

INTRODUCTION

You Are My Son, with Whom I Am Well-Pleased

This book is written specifically for sons of toxic mothers. You or someone you love may or may not be aware of the negative effects of his mother's abuses. Not everyone understands that parenting can be better, that mothering can be better. Survivors of caustic mothering many times can't even reflect on their personal, internal workings and external life habits in response to their mother's dysfunction. Life with a toxic mother can wound and damage a child to the very core. That kind of destruction impairs us in ways unimaginable, and the ultimate conclusion is hopelessness and helplessness.

It's not fair, kind, or compassionate that when we finally grow up and (hopefully) escape our toxic mothers, we must deal with the collateral damage for the rest of our lives. Our mother may not have been Cruella de Vil, but she sure wasn't Molly Weasley or Ma (Caroline) Ingalls, either. Somehow, in our youthful ignorance, we simply grow up to do the best we can. When we discover our personal and relational struggles as adults, we all deal with them in different ways, we all need different kinds of help, some of us heal and become quite productive but we don't know how or why. Some of us are aware of the pain, but handle it ourselves, keeping every outside influence away—healthy and destructive—but finding ourselves alone or stuck in our quest to make it.

I always knew something was askew with my mother, even in my childhood years. But, like most children, I thought my experiences were universal, convinced that my peers felt the same way I did, that every way I reacted to my outside environment was filtered somehow through my mother's approval lens. I didn't know that independence could be taught without shaming. I didn't know how important it is that parents encourage us to have healthy friends. I grieved when I realized my mother's unconditional love was conditional. That was just the way life worked. We played by her rules. And, she had many rules—spoken and unspoken—that I had to obey to be rewarded with another day with her as my mother. She was my mother who must be pleased at all cost to ourselves.

I'm Not a Child Anymore

This is the best way I can describe my childhood and youth. Of course, my mother provided me tender moments, teaching moments, material necessities, and more. I acknowledge that I am just as responsible for my reaction to her physical, emotional, and mental manipulation as she is for that manipulation. I am just as responsible for my own toxicity as she is for hers. But as children, it's hard to put a finger on our mother's modus operandi. Boys and girls alike internalize our parents' rules-to-live-by. We also create our own in response to those rules. Fathers can be toxic, too, imposing inappropriate rules-to-live-by onto their children and insisting in harmful ways that their children obey.

However, we as adult children of a toxic parent must learn to advocate for ourselves in the context of each parent individually. I wrote this book to help sons of toxic mothers to begin to heal in the context of untangling ourselves from the abuse and dysfunction we have experienced from our mothers. One parent at a time, one of her toxic rules-to-live-by at a time.

Every relationship between a son and his mother is different and every one of us has responded to our mothers in unique ways. But, when a mother is toxic, we sons are thrown together to discover what works for us. From interviewing men for this book, leading men's retreats, personal experience, and actual research data, I've discovered we men really do come up short when attempting to sort out the condition of our life in response to our toxic mothers, and it lingers and infects us into our adulthood.

Help on the Horizon?

Before sons begin to seek healing from such abuses as those illustrated in this book, we must first acknowledge that we need help to see beyond the horizon. Fortunately, for years women have been finding support addressing this deep wounding with their mothers. It's a different story for men who are the collateral damage of such dysfunction. Whatever the reason men may need special help to heal, we as a society benefit when we guide these men to receive that help. Whether you are a son who is wondering how to become a better person, a mother who may have spewed your toxicity onto your sons, or the loved one of a son in search of healing, we can benefit from understanding the process recommended in this book and applying it to our personal situation. It is up to you to take the first step to understand that process in order to create your own customized plan to live, love, and be loved well.

While there are many ways to identify, describe, and heal from toxicity, we sons grow up with an innate desire to be virtuous men of integrity who love others and who are loved well. Our lives deteriorate when we stop living out that desire. This book takes the reader through the entire cyclical process of healing when we find ourselves in a vortex of stagnancy, shame, futility, anger, self-hate, destructive relationships, addictive behaviors, loneliness, anxiety, personal/professional/relational failure, and much more.

The process begins by defining clearly what rules-to-live-by are and their role in helping us heal. We design our lives by creating, adapting, internalizing, and executing rules that we believe will bring us life. We assume that if we obey these rules and others follow suit, our lives will be made better, more complete, superior. It is when we or others impose those rules onto others in inappropriate ways that we spiral into the world of dysfunction and toxicity. Identifying the influence and impact these rules have on our personal lives and life goals becomes the beginning of a structured process to design our own path of healing, which may or may not include professional counseling, distancing ourselves from our mothers and other toxic people, joining a social or special interest group, finding a mentor, mentoring younger men, reading a book, self-reflection, setting boundaries, learning what it means to love others boldly, and so much more.

I believe society does not overtly encourage men to heal and nurture their inner-child the same way it does for women. With a toxic mother, we sons are left somehow to figure it all out on our own. We can't see the hopeful and helpful ways to focus beyond the horizon. We want to enjoy healthy relationships with other people, but we don't know how. We have no positive role model. And both toxic mothers and society itself send mixed signals of how and if we are to maintain our dysfunctional relationship with the very woman we are to revere for giving us life.

Does This Sound Familiar?

In true toxic fashion, our mother, dysfunctional whether in word or deed, reminds us consistently how we've failed. "You haven't figured out anything in your life. Why can't you pay your mortgage this month?" she might say. Or, "You still don't know what you want to be when you grow up." Or, "You can't keep a girlfriend for more than a month without one of you bailing for some strange reason." And finally, "Why don't you come to visit me more often? Are you scared? Don't you even care that I'm lonely and hurting over here?" Guilt, guilt, guilt.

If you are a man reading this, I can imagine the echoes going off in your head. I have heard them, too, and I still hear some today. In trying to escape the heavy darkness we carry, we attempt to live our lives, hoping for the best but not really knowing or acknowledging what that may be. Our natural impulse to love and respect our mother wages war against the misery and pain she hurls at us. We create coping mechanisms to help us get through a day or a week—or a visit with our toxic moms. I call these mechanisms the three B's: *bumble*, *blaze*, and *back away*. We *bumble* through the relationship intentionally or unconsciously oblivious to how we affect her or we *blaze* through our life consciously manipulating and controlling her and our environment to protect ourselves and those we love or we *back away* from her when she pushes us to an uncomfortable place—

any place—for whatever reason and retreat to wherever we can or want.

Ideally, her tenderness, care, emotional maturity, and selflessness should provide the freedom for a child to grow into a loving, tender, selfless person, but we know how dysfunctional things become in a family when a mother constantly criticizes, controls, shames, and manipulates her children. With a passive aggression, these "adult" women invalidate their children's emotions and disrespect boundaries children don't even know they should have.[1] In reacting to these sorts of abuses from our mothers, we end up rejecting her demanding rules-to-live-by but suffer in silence. But we also don't know how to keep our own rules from taking us down the path to becoming toxic ourselves.

To make matters worse, in today's male-bashing arena of political correctness, bumbling, blazing, blaming and backing away are simply considered weak male attributes—misogyny, toxic masculinity, or whatever woke thing might strip men from their ability to reclaim the power their toxic mother so craftily stole. We men don't feel the same freedom to express our feelings, especially when it comes to our opinion of other women. Some men are conditioned to stuff those feelings and plunge themselves into other activity—wholesome or not. We might become workaholics or apathetic freeloaders. We might womanize or express confusion over our gender and sexuality, and shut ourselves off to outside influences, or input simply out of shame and fear.[2]

Sharing your concerns over a toxic mother has the potential to expose yourself as a weak mama's boy, a wuss, ungrateful, selfish, and so much more. We are tempted to discard or at least hide these feelings, which also sets us up to practice the same kind of toxicity with those we love. The cycle continues. Lots of research indicates that men have unique obstacles to overcome if they are to seek mental health care.[3] We easily feel trapped, afraid to assess our lives and our hearts in search of freedom from the prison cell—the prison cell where our toxic mother holds the key.

So . . . What Do We Need to Escape?

The first step of the process in this book is to identify the power of rules-to-live-by in our lives. The second step is to create and practice new rules that help us to become a virtuous, loving man of integrity. Last, we step out into our life with our new rules and live freely, joyously, lovingly, and humbly. And we perform well when there is a plan or process in place that removes the obstacles we may be experiencing. This book will help you make that plan. While on the path to healing, we need a way to measure how well we are healing too. I provide a tangible and powerful way to self-assess our progress as our lives mature, evolve, and heal one rule at a time.

We need a way to examine—even heal—our relationship with our toxic mother where we can emerge unscathed on the other side, equipped to love and be loved, serve and be served, and express ourselves as the free and unique individuals we are. We need a place where we encourage and are encouraged by other men, learning from each other as iron sharpens iron. We need to find safety in exploring what's right and wrong, properly and safely righting our wrongs while personally and even collectively celebrating our victories.

Is That All?

The solution is not that easy. It is a process not a product, a process of moving on with our lives that helps us grow stronger and healthier along the way. I've been on the path for thirty-seven years and still going. And, we do not need to struggle with this alone. I love to gather groups of men to go on weekend retreats in order to deepen our faith, friendship-building skills, and fellowship, and I have discovered one thing for sure about men. We all need help reflecting on our lives in any and every category, and in particular our relationships with our toxic mothers. This book helps streamline this process.

My toxic mother tried her hardest to bring me down to the lowest point she could in order to beat me—physically, emotionally, and mentally—into compliance with her grand but secret plan for my life to benefit hers. Read the stories in this book. Every one of them is 100 percent true with a few details changed to protect the living and innocent. In my desperation to escape my mother's toxicity, I unknowingly brought similar toxicity with me to college, to my career, and to my wife, children, and friends.

At rock bottom, I sought professional help to begin untangling myself from my mother's control. For the most part, counseling helped (and is still helping), and I hope by reading this book you can also take advantage of trusted professional advice mentioned or reflected in this book to heal yourself and perhaps your relationship with your toxic mother. Had I read this book as a younger man, I would have had a tool—a process—to take life one experience at a time and become a better, more loving person. I am not a professional psychologist or therapist; I'm an educator. In spite of all the dysfunction I've experienced, I have discovered God's calling on my life—to inspire others to learn. And this includes how to live and love with freedom. In this book, I detail each step of the process to help us as sons of toxic mothers—and anyone else who reads it—to design personal action plans for becoming the virtuous man of integrity we choose.

This book will help you whether your toxic mother is alive or not. It can help you gain insight and acquire tools to confront your very personal circumstances and issues. The end goal is your personal healing, which allows you to fulfill your life calling and mission on your own terms, perhaps moving on enough to love your toxic mother in her saddest and most needy times. The real-life illustrations allow you to explore the action points in this guide safely and vicariously. Understanding another son's relationship with his toxic mother can help you be part of a larger redemptive story to heal yourself, affecting every one of your relationships on this side of heaven and then to move on to become the man you choose to be.

And, as you heal like this book suggests, you will encourage others to begin healing too. I hope my story and this book encourage you to take the first steps toward healing. But, I am not the only one with this success story. Many men, some of whom have attended my retreats and some who attend virtual support groups, have gone even further down the path. Let their stories inspire you too. You can find out more at my website: www.guyarcuri.com. When you encounter any concept or action point that interests you, do your research. Use the book, especially its last chapter, to find sources that help you personally and proactively design a plan for healing.

The Book

The three sections in *Toxic Mothers: A Son's Guide to Healing and Moving on* each represent a body of research, wisdom, and personal experience to help you consolidate not only what to consider while healing but how, where, and why. Each section highlights principles and practices with which to filter your approach to healing yourself and your relationship with your toxic mother. The first section, **Men and Their Relationships with Toxic Mothers**, reveals the unique nature of the relationship between a toxic mother and her son. The snapshot story in Chapter 1 sets the stage to learn to examine both your toxic mother's life and your own. Afterward, you'll discover the process by which we become toxic and then a new process to set ourselves up for healing and moving on.

The second section, **Breaking Down the Healing Process**, provides many strategies to heal very specific areas of our life. By consolidating volumes of information into memorable packages, it answers the question, "What can and should I heal?" All efforts must first and foremost be directed toward ourselves if we are going to make positive changes in a relationship. Section Two broadens and details each step of the book's suggested healing process to help sons take charge of their lives. By Section Two you will have reflected on your core values and rules by which you want to live in healthy relationships with anyone, not just your toxic mother.

Section 3, **Healing Tips**, helps you embrace sustainable relationship-building frameworks that promise to carry you through the healing process in ways that celebrate the good times, happiness, inspirations, and joy as much as encourages you in the midst of the sorrow, pain, cruelty, and dysfunction that surface while intentionally interacting with your toxic mother.

The strategies suggested in Section Three apply the research from counseling and psychology experts and provide a technique or activity that will open doors for you to practice the health and freedom you are developing. Finally, in Chapter 13 I provide my final word, which includes describing various kinds of therapy and resources for readers to consider and acknowledgments of people who have walked with me in my healing.

Immediately following is an annotated set of endnotes that comment further on some of the ideas throughout the book to help you explore your individual path to healing and moving on.

Through hard work, I was able to delight in and with my mother during the last six months of her life, when she needed me most, fighting terminal, aggressive metastatic cancer. My hope is that by reading this book, your healing will come faster and more deeply than mine. Change is possible. Love is possible. Healing is possible. Use this guide as the tool it was meant to be. You will come out on the other side of toxic to find Grace and Truth and Freedom.

SECTION 1

Men and Their Relationships with Toxic Mothers

CHAPTER 1

MY STORY: GRIEF OVER WHAT COULD HAVE BEEN

In December of 2018, my mother gave me a special Christmas present. Her ocular melanoma, one of the most aggressive cancers ever, had metastasized, spread to her liver, and she was going to refuse treatment. She said the doctor gave her three to four months. *I didn't believe a word she said.* She had lied to me her whole life, and within the last two months, I had exposed her for lying to me about her health, her financial situation, her independence, her blindness, her eating habits, and so much more, including pitting me against my own brother with the craftiest but most typical of her manipulation.

She was living in Tucson, Arizona, and I as far away as I could from her and her toxic world . . . North Carolina. I had consciously chosen to live apart from my family of origin since the age of nineteen. During my early adult years, I grieved what could have been, but with few tools to navigate life on my own, I found myself drawn back into her venomous world over and over.

I had not squandered the distance I had so intentionally placed between us, though. I had been training for this "Christmas gift" my whole life. This moment rose out of the ashes of her abuse, and I, with no anger, resentment, or even self-righteousness, simply responded, "Well, thanks for telling me. Is there something <u>you</u> want to do or somewhere <u>you</u> want to go while you still have time? I guess I'm asking if you have a bucket list." Notice I did not say, "Is there anything you want <u>me</u> to do for <u>you</u>?" I had learned never to open that door! She would have snatched that opportunity like a hawk snatches an injured rabbit! But, instead of talons, she would have broken me down with her shame and anger and lies.

She replied in a matter-of-fact way, like she had just rubbed a genie's lamp. "I have three wishes. I want to go to Pennsylvania and Ohio to say goodbye to my friends and family there. I want to fly first class, and I want to go to Disney World." I thought, "Easy enough!" But before I could reply, she interjected with crackling voice and tears I've come to ignore, "And I don't want to die alone, but I know your brother won't even answer my calls." I knew that familiar triangulation and guilt-provoking commentary, and I easily read between the lines. I had sought counseling and therapy and read hundreds of books on how to detect the demand behind her "sweet" statements. She wanted me to be with her while she died. I responded, "Done!" Without flinching, with the utmost of **confidence**, I had just agreed to fulfill my toxic mother's bucket list and be with her as she voluntarily wastes away to nothing.

Notice, too, I did not say with *love* or *compassion*, but I said *confidence*. I knew I had healed and moved on enough to enter a world I had spent a lifetime escaping. To a third-party observer, my mother was a "sweet old lady." Welcoming, fun, adventurous, and even loving. To her circle of friends and extended family, she certainly had endured pain and suffering in raising her children, surviving horrific abuse from her father and equal neglect from her mother, tolerating a chronically adulterous husband with whom she chose to remain, rehabilitating her daughter from the depths of drug addiction, mental illness, and brain damage, raising that daughter's two children, losing that daughter to hospital negligence, saying goodbye to her husband of fifty-five years, serving as caregiver while her fiancée died, and more. But, all along the way, she ensnared us, her *immediate* family, into her world of dysfunction, manipulation, and abuse.

My confidence led me to take charge of this bucket list/hospice mission. And, while in the dungeons of accomplishing this quest, I would write . . . write to keep my sanity . . . write to dam up the flood of emotions and memories she would conjure with her very being . . . write to bind my pain and suffering onto paper to at once be liberated upon completion, not only upon the completion of this writing, but of her life as well.

Did You Say Grief?

I had no time to grieve what might have been, but I couldn't escape the deluge of competing sentiments. The grief was there. I've spent my whole adult life shielding myself from her masterfully camouflaged toxicity, and we had both missed out on developing a loving and mutually respectful relationship. During her time in hospice, I began to journal about whatever surfaced as I spent every other week in Arizona. I was naïve and delusional that others could heal and move on simply by knowing my sad and pathetic story. I wrote intensely and prolifically; something redemptive ought to come out of this bizarre memoir of contempt. But after her death, I plunged deeply into a cruel and relentless vengeance that ate at my soul. My brother, whose hate for her still rings in my ears, died thirty-two days after her. He was my last hope of speaking freely about our shared horrors we—and only we two—called "living in Hazel World."

Our mother, Hazel Arcuri, lived in that Hazel World alone, sharing with the outside world how wonderful our life with her had been. But, with my brother gone and I a complete orphan, I was left with my own rage and guilt and confusion. So, I changed directions with the tone and content of this book. I do not hate my mother. As her son, I wanted to love her. Instead of grieving what could have been, I wanted to live my life more proactively, as I have been learning to do for so many years.

My goal here is not to destroy her character posthumously. I am not vengeful. I have worked intentionally at becoming an encourager. I am not afraid to love others. I want to help other sons develop a healthy relationship with their toxic mothers by putting into practice conscious and noble efforts to reclaim their lives. I *do* grieve the lost time with my mother both because of her toxicity and my extreme rejection of everything Hazel World. But, I have replaced that pain and anger with hope. I cannot provide hope, encouragement, or strength to anyone if I am seeking revenge toward anyone else. Faith, hope, and love, and the greatest of these is love!

I needed faith to break away from my own bitterness. I found hope at the end of this writing, and that hope came from letting you know my story of learning to love my mother all over again.

Perfect love casts out fear and desperation. When I was younger, I was afraid of my toxic mother, and I chose to respond in desperate and impulsive ways, attempting to orchestrate her happiness and earn her acceptance, something she was incapable of experiencing. There is no need to mourn what could have been in this situation. I have learned to release the fear and grief and replace them with something new: love. Now I have a new focus for writing and living. I hope you can find that too.

CHAPTER 2

MEN, FEAR, AND GRIEF

Today, psychologists readily diagnose and treat toxic mothers and victimized children.[4] They even provide clear steps for adult children to heal from the predictable effects. This book channels that advice and more. But, what keeps a son from beginning the work to untangle from his disheartening mother? What do sons do instead of confronting the dysfunction head-on? Unique factors go into a son's decision to abstain from any therapeutic intervention. As men we must first face this general truth before looking at the specifics. Fear forms the roadblock for most men in two ways. First, men fear decision-making as it relates to the life-giving mother who raised them. Second, men fear being paralyzed by this indecision and react strongly but naively to being stuck in a relationship with their toxic mother.[5] Let's examine both kinds of fears.

Fear of the Unknown

Men are conditioned to fear what they cannot see or know. We fear what Mom will say when we tell her no, for example. We fear the surge of negative emotions that comes when her toxicity is being hurled at us like darts. Once, when my parents were visiting my family, I waited until the very last minute to tell them I would be taking us out to dinner. I feared my mother—what she would say and how she would react. All week she was brewing some witch-like potion, but I couldn't figure out what. Over and over she kept saying,

"Guy, I can fix us all leftovers for dinner. You know how well I can whip up something great."

I exercised my right to remain silent as long as I could. I couldn't tell her that no one in my family ate leftovers except me. That would reinforce her overwhelming judgment that my family and I are entitled, rich snobs. My whole life she beat into my heart the need to be frugal, because only rich people waste food. I certainly couldn't condone that. My wife left work early assuming we would go out to dinner. Our children were on their way home from sports and tutoring. So, I snapped. "Mom, I'm going to take us out to dinner so we can have time to talk and not have to clean up." The cauldron bubbled over with trouble and toil.

"Guy! Again? We're going out to eat *again*? All you do is *waste* money, and you're all going to get *fat* eating out so much. Your kids are going to be so *spoiled* and never learn how to cook. You think your house is still too *cluttered* for us all to eat here, don't you. Is that it? I already offered to clean it all up. You're just too *lazy* to cook and clean and enjoy your own home. You're *spoiling* your kids just like all rich people do with your maid and your yard man."

My fear kept me from confronting the truths and desires that are just as valid as hers, but she had little respect for either. I would have loved to talk about how we greatly appreciate the woman who cleans our house, and our yard man has taught me more truth, wisdom, and faith than she had my entire life. But instead, I blamed my decision on my wife for being tired and wanting to go out to her favorite restaurant.

Men also fear the unknown possibility of being exposed. Will stating what I want or need open me up to hurt or humiliation? Will admitting I am wrong expose me as incompetent or stupid? Will confronting my issues with my toxic mother allow her or others to see me as weak? Dependent? Needy? Ignorant? Ungrateful?

At nineteen years old, I left my home never to return, but was regularly drawn back to experiment whether a relationship with my mother was even possible. The only thing I needed from my parents was a signature on my student loan, and I was out of their lives forever. I never asked her for anything, even as we had kids and secured profitable careers. I was too afraid. When I did ask, she would prey on my vulnerability and remind me how much I disappointed her or how selfish I was or what a foolish decision I had made.

Me? Make Myself Vulnerable to a Tyrant?

After years of her badgering me to let her spend time with my kids, I paid for my entire extended family to vacation together at the beach. It was a busy time for me, but I thought it would be a great way to have my kids interact with my parents on neutral ground. I was in the process of applying for tenure at a university, and time was running out for me to submit my work. I asked my parents for one favor. Marie (my wife) was out of the country for an extended period of time, and I desperately needed childcare the week after our vacation. So, I asked them if they could do that for me. It would also be a great way for them to spend time with my children themselves since my mother continually told me I was intentionally keeping them from her. They agreed with delight, insisting on driving my children in their conversion van from Delaware to North Carolina after the vacation, which, in turn, would free me up to fly home and begin the arduous task of compiling my tenure documents.

I told them I would pay for any expense they incurred. After the vacation, my mother came up to me while I was packing my kids in their van and she said, "Guy, your dad has to return a leaf blower to our neighbor so we're going to drop you and the kids off at the airport early. We're not going to North Carolina. We'll do it another time." They dumped me, our luggage, my daughter, her stroller, my son, his car seat at the airport eight hours early with a simple "goodbye." I hadn't bought a single ticket for my children on my flight. I made myself vulnerable this one time twenty years after escaping the anxiety of living with my toxic mother, and nothing had changed. Grandchildren or a leaf blower?

We fear the unknown consequences of our decisions. We might fear our toxic mothers retaliating for something out of our control, unknown, or brand-new. These kinds of unpredictable moms threaten to sever ties with their sons emotionally, physically, financially, socially, and more. We sons second-guess our own importance and validity when we fear our mothers will even the score if we go against their wishes. Did my mother deny me her childcare to punish me for something I had not noticed or that I had inflicted on her unknowingly? I'll never know. Should I ever again mention that I need something from her? Would I lose my relationship with my father, brother, or sister if she cuts me off in one of her toxic rampages? The paralysis is real.

Men Acting Out: Fear of Indecision

When we men find ourselves stripped of options, lacking the freedom and independence to express ourselves or do what we believe to be good or right, we sometimes panic. Our reaction might be appropriate or not. That is life. But, most of the time, men burst out in desperation to do *something* that defines us. So, we make large-scale or extreme decisions, many times impulsively, fearing our whole life will be consumed by our toxic mother's tentacles if we don't. My brother and I both experienced moments when we made rash, immature choices to do something . . . anything . . . to get away from the harsh environment in search of our own identities.

My Brother's Moment

My brother had bumbled, blazed, and backed away from our toxic mother for two more years than I. After graduating from high school, she nagged him about his drinking, his study habits, and, worst of all, his girlfriend. This girlfriend was two years older than he, much more mature in some ways, and Mark ended up at her place overnight more often than our mother thought appropriate. She nagged him incessantly about the immorality and shaming appearance it projected onto him and our family. While Mark was in and out of living at my parents' house, however, they allowed our older sister to bring home a drug-addicted bum who mooched off my parents, slept in the same bed with my sister, stole money out of my sister's bank account, and performed felonies I'm not comfortable sharing in this book.

My parents' hypocrisy, especially my mother's, drove my brother to escape our mother's badgering him over how immoral he was with his girlfriend. He impulsively moved out of our house and in with his girlfriend against my mother's wishes or knowledge. He simply needed relief in whatever form he could find from our mother's oppression and demoralizing. He disengaged from my mother altogether. He buried himself in alcohol, his glory days, and staying very far away from my mother. He also filled his calendar year-round with activity that kept him away from her. He worked incessantly. He plunged into coaching, inspiring thousands of young people to be the best they could while enjoying their life: baseball, soccer, football, diving, pole vaulting. Over his two-day funeral services, more than eight hours of people lined up to pay their respects to a man who wanted to validate someone else instead of validating himself at their expense. He had acted impulsively on his desperate decision so he could define himself as a fun-loving family man and coach. We'll see, as in my moment, that turning ourselves away from one dysfunction without informed ways to heal and create healthier patterns is not a sustainable solution.

My Moment

To set the stage for my own desperate life-changing decision, I must go back a year earlier when I became a Christian. Immaturely and perhaps with malice, I announced my complete rejection of Catholicism and that now I was a born-again, Bible-believing, evangelical Christian, as was Marie, my then girlfriend. My parents were devastated and my mother made it clear that I was not respecting the "family morals." This bumbling, blazing, and backing away from my mother resulted in impulsive decisions and reactions very similar to my brother's. It culminated when I told my mother I loved Marie and would probably marry her . . . at age nineteen!

She did not express shock at our ages. She did not question the financial feasibility of such an action. She did not mention the blast of anti-Catholic sentiment I had ranted the year before. She simply asked, "Guy, is she Catholic?" I genuinely loved my girlfriend, and at nineteen years old, I was wavering on whether to tell my mother or not. But, I was more afraid NOT to act on my decision than I was afraid of this interrogation I would get from my mother. She challenged my decisions with no consideration of my personal interests or boundaries.

Mom somehow still construed Marie's Southern heritage with the two facts that Marie was rich and Protestant, and both made Mom's toxicity boil with an unwarranted bitterness that I was being torn away from my "roots." Mom had not been to church in over five years, but that day, she lectured me about how Marie would have to convert to Catholicism, we could only get married in a Catholic church, and everything else Catholic. I chose right then and there I would marry Marie, finish college, and never return home. That was MY moment! My world was never going to survive an encounter with Hazel World.

It was extreme, and I tempered that commitment as I matured, but my desperate decision to reject my life at home made as much collateral damage for me and my family as my mother's toxicity did to me. I own that. In the process, though, I defined myself as the academic Christian who will never have the support of his family. It was all up to me. I would never make myself vulnerable to her again.

A Son's Moment

People are rarely taught how to handle fear, whether they recognize it in themselves or not. Therapists help women and men alike address the paralyzing effects of fear and phobia, and all the advice is helpful for all. But, research might misconstrue the basic differences between a man's and woman's reactions to fear and toxic mothers. It is true that slightly fewer men than women suffer from the effect of their toxic mothers. Elisabetta Franzoso, a *female* therapist specializing in healthy relationships, explains that there are

> more growing opportunities to separate men and women [to help them heal from their toxic mothers]. Men and women are after all, always seen in a separate light—no less because of the surmounting research on our different needs, and as John Gray revealed in his popular TEDTalk, different brains.[6]

But later, Franzoso simply implicates a male-dominated society for the woes of any child's struggle with a suppressive mother and generalizes about her negative effects. How is a man supposed to heal from his toxic mother when society unfairly makes him part of the problem? However, Rick Belden, 2017, an author-researcher "helping men who feel stuck get their lives moving," uses his *male* voice to highlight the unique issues facing men.[7]

Why do men avoid their Mother Wounds?

Awareness and acknowledgment of his Mother Wound is typically a huge taboo for a man . . . Most sons have been trained and are expected to be protective of their mother and her feelings at all costs. Fear can be a significant deterrent as well. For many men . . . there is nothing more frightening (or unthinkable) than looking into their own Mother Wounds. I know my Father Wound well. It hurts but does not scare me. My Mother Wound terrifies me. It feels like a pit from which there is no return.

As I have shown before in this chapter, fear is a unique feature of a son's response to his toxic mother. And Belden adds another: grief.

Doing the work

. . . it's taken me many years to begin to move into my own Mother Wound work fully, and I still find it very challenging. The hardest part, aside from the fear I mentioned, has been the surprisingly deep well of grief I've found in myself as I've moved into the emotional energy associated with the wound. I had a sense it was there, but having a sense of it and actually moving into it (and feeling it) are two very different things. It is, perhaps, the most powerful grief of all: the grief of a child. And it's been driving and influencing my relationships [of all kinds] . . . unconsciously and often indirectly, for my entire life.

My story in Chapter 1 highlights the role grief has played in my attempt to find meaning and healing for a lost childhood and youth. As the innocence of an abused child transforms into a self-protective fear of the unknown and fear of indecision, sons lose the ability to see their own agency in dealing with their toxic mothers. It's important, then, to learn how to see what goes on in our own hearts.

CHAPTER 3

TOXICITY: HERS AND OURS

The road to recovery begins with looking at yourself. To heal, then, we must first ask ourselves, "Do we accept responsibility for the choices we've made in our own life?" Are we willing to look at the conscious and subconscious decisions we've made that brought us to this present state and examine the impact they've had on our health and those whom we love and with whom we interact? As an educator, I know how difficult it is for people to self-assess. People struggle to look introspectively into their own hearts, motivations, and life frameworks. Their philosophical, spiritual, psychological, and mental states affect them subconsciously.

This chapter will help you dig into your own psyche by understanding the nature and function of toxicity. That way, you can begin to assess your own toxicity to help you transform into the better person you envision. You will definitively also have to identify the origins of your mother's toxicity. In my own experience, being able to detect and label the toxicity coming at me by my mother was crucial to my being able to react in ways that loved her and maintained my own dignity and integrity, a goal I had set early on in my own therapy to heal from my mother's escapades.

So, what does it mean to be toxic, and how does that relate to your path of healing?

> ### Toxicity
>
> *Toxicity is one person placing demands (our personal set of rules for the way life should be) on others and then insisting in destructive ways that those demands be met.* Both the demands and the insistence can be seen or unseen, passive and/or aggressive, public or private, internal or external. No matter how toxic people choose to poison their victim, what matters most is that the victim acquiesce. This general definition of *toxic* will become helpful later. With its broad application to overlapping fields in the mental health clinical world, "toxic" can define a wide spectrum of behaviors and traits.[8] Clarification is needed. Let's examine some of the research to detail a few of the identifiable traits of a toxic person. For purposes of this book, we will use the research that describes toxic mothers.

What Do the Experts Say?

According to BetterHelp.com,[9] a team of mental health professional experts, "[a] toxic mother is a mother who consistently ignores your stated boundaries, withholds love, invalidates your feelings in any way, [and] displays toxic traits." BetterHelp.com then lists and explains toxic traits for all people, which I consider to fall into two broad categories. Specifically, two mental states must be considered in order for both son and toxic mother to heal themselves.

The first is *motive*. It is crucial to reflect on your own demands on your mother and the motivation behind your interactions with her. It is just as crucial to consider your mother's motivation behind her demands and insistence. Second, a son's *perception*, or personal understanding, of his mother's toxicity is the beginning of self-awareness and mindfulness in this mother-son relationship. But, a son must try as much as possible to discover what his mother means by each and every demand he identifies in his assessment and analysis. He must listen and watch during safe moments and interactions. Understanding BettherHelp's traits opens the door for a son to explore the motives and perceptions while exposing the nuances of a mother's toxicity.[10]

As will be seen in Chapter 6, understanding these traits as categories helps you ask the right questions and therefore react with intention, health, safety, and even compassion. Keep in mind that it takes climbing intentional steps in a constant cycle to go from identifying toxic traits to becoming a healing man of integrity who loves others well. The following is an elaboration of each of those questions as they relate to BetterHelp's traits identified by these bulleted points and italics. And, with those reflection questions, I offer some explanation and illustrations.

- *Constant criticism*: What is Mom specifically criticizing? When does she consistently criticize? What does she think you need to do or be instead? How do you react when she criticizes? What, if anything, will make her stop criticizing you in this area? It is easy to understand that your mother is critical. But, to begin healing, it is important to map when and how she criticizes. In addition, when you identify sanely and clearly Mom's criticisms, you can think rationally and react in ways that strip her of incapacitating you. My mother constantly criticized me for keeping a cluttered house. She said she just couldn't stay in a place with so many stacks of papers and clothes. We had an old house with little storage space, but that was not the true excuse. The fact was, my wife and I had time-consuming careers, difficulty having children, and had grown quite accustomed to our stacks. When I had had enough of my mother's criticism, I remained silent. The next time my parents came to visit me in my hometown, upon arrival I went out to meet them, got into their car, and guided them to a nearby hotel where I had reserved them a room. We had a delightful time.

- *Controlling behavior*: What does Mom want to accomplish by making you do one thing or keeping you from doing another? Is it for selfish reasons? What are her assumptions around the behavior? Does your reaction reflect a fight or flight response? How are you reacting? Are you controlled? Is *your* reaction trying to control your mother in return? If you are reading this, you are old enough to choose your own life path. By examining individual controlling behaviors in specific situations, you begin to sort out what is important, what battles are important to enter, fight, or win. Perhaps she controls where and how you interact with your family and friends. If, for example, she doesn't invite you to a birthday celebration because she is mad at something you've done or said or represented, that does not stop you from celebrating that birthday in another way. When you react to Mom's controlling behavior by letting it distract you from your life goals and purpose, you will lose the sense that you have much more control than you think. It's up to you to discover what's important to you and how you can pursue it on your terms.

- *Guilt-tripping and manipulation*: What angers you when you feel obligated or manipulated by your mom? Can you live happily without doing or having what it is she baits you with as she makes you comply? Our daughter didn't speak until she was twenty-six months old. We were concerned but hopeful it was just a developmental thing. Our speech therapist said we were simply being anxious first-time parents, but she also told us to speak to her as much as we could in turn-taking fashion where we expect a verbal response.

When I mustered enough courage to bring her to my mother's house for the first time, my mother oohed and ahhhed, but, when I interacted verbally with my daughter, especially when I was trying to discipline her, Mom would shake her head in disgust. So, stupidly, I asked what was wrong, and she said, "Guy, you give her way too much attention. She's going to be a spoiled brat by the time she's three if all you do is talk to her. She needs a spanking. You need to put her in her place before she takes advantage of you. You can't talk to a two-year-old." While I was there, my mother had manipulated me enough to doubt every time I spoke to my daughter. Even more confusing, in front of me she publicly bragged to her friends what a great dad I was. I felt limited and feared I was doing everything wrong as a parent. I was responsible for my guilty response, but my mother is the one who knowingly pushed those buttons.

- *Humiliation*: Do you believe what she is saying when she shames you? Why or why not? Does she believe it? How do you know? What do you believe or know about yourself that contradicts her shaming words and deeds? How have you let Mom's toxic shame convince you of its truth? Think of the above scenario. As a young, first-time parent, it was pretty easy to tip my emotional scale to the humiliation and frustration of parenting skills.

- *Invalidation of your emotions*: Are you able to identify your own emotions accurately? Are your emotions valid? How do you know? Why do you think Mom is preying on your emotions? What are her understandings of the emotions she is attempting to invalidate in your life? My mother must have known that one of the effects of her toxic behaviors forced me to dissociate from my emotions. I now know it takes conscious effort for me to be in tune with my emotions in real time. Part of that is due to my mother's constant invalidation of what I was actually feeling.

As a child we were never allowed to drink carbonated beverages. Yet, my parents would throw elaborate parties with dozens of half-full 2-liter bottles left over, lining the hallway. One morning, I woke up early and sampled all the bottles, one at a time. My mother caught me.

"What do you think you're doing, Guy?"

"I didn't drink any!" An outright lie.

"So, not only are you stealing the soda, you're also a liar?"

"Mom, I really wanted some soda."

"Well, why should I give you anything you want? You obviously can't even tell the truth."

To this day, as an adult, I drink soda over water simply because I'm free to choose. But, it took a great deal of counseling to trust the idea that it is OK to express what I feel and want without the dismissal of my emotions.

- *Passive aggression*: How does it help you to know if Mom's victimization of you is passive-aggressive? When you feel threatened, what are the common scenarios? What do you do when you feel threatened? How would you define passive aggression? What does it look like coming from you? At you? Can you or your mother de-escalate when things get out of control?[11]

My mother constantly guilted me about how I would never go to their home with my wife and children. Mom said I was too rich and educated to be associated with my parents. So, out of guilt, I would haul my family in a car or plane five hundred miles to Pennsylvania. They had an open invitation to come to my house, had nothing but time, but never once visited me here unless I begged. At their home, my father would watch TV during every waking hour, and my mother would either shame me about how I was "spoiling" my children with freedoms and material things or she inappropriately shamed my children with her "discipline," or she gave the majority of her attention to my sister's children whom she helped raise.

After realizing her toxic guilt, shame, and manipulation were not worth the trip, I simply told her I was not going to go to Pennsylvania unless there was a plan and that we would not be staying at their home. They were always welcome to come to my home, and I would pay their way. Her reaction? She said, "Well, that just proves my point! You are just embarrassed to be around us." I diffused her passive aggression. She would say how she missed my children but make my life hell when I visited her or she visited me.

- *Disrespectful of personal boundaries:*[12] What does Mom think she is gaining by crossing boundaries? Does she act entitled to your personal information (mail, packages, dating updates, salary, or anything of a personal nature?) What kind of boundaries have you placed on your mother? Does she know you are trying to set boundaries? Why or why not? To illustrate this, consider one seemingly light-hearted story. When we were dating, my wife, Marie, surprised me a few weeks after my first year of college. She flew up to Philadelphia, got my sister to pick her up at the Lancaster train station, and casually walked into my parents' house. It was amazing! I had just finished making her a gift (a pom-pom doll named Matthew), and we immediately found touristy activity to spend time together. When Marie went to bed, my mother grabbed me by the arm to motion that I not go to my own room, but that I stay with her "to talk."

"Guy, I gotta ask you this because I'm your mother. Does Marie have an eating disorder?"

"What? No. What makes you say that?"

"Well, I was going through her suitcase while you were outside, and I found a whole bag of Brach's Cinnamon Disks candy. And, now they're gone! She's eaten every one of them!"

"Mom, she gave them to me! They're my favorite candy, and maybe *I* have an eating disorder! I've already eaten half the bag!" (Note my own passive aggression in return.) I continued, "Besides, it's none of your business what she had in her suitcase. That's her property and you shouldn't be rummaging through it."

Now, let it be known that the Arcuri children would be

beaten with the bristle or hard side of a brush (our choice) if *we* opened up *her* mail!

She responded, "I'm your mother and I have a right to do whatever I want here! You remember that! You are just a guest in my house, and I don't have to give a reason for looking at anything that's in my house."

I let it go! She had no sense of boundaries, but I knew she was fishing for a way to get this "Protestant" woman out of my life. Interestingly, my mother made Marie's life miserable by constantly complaining that Marie chose **not** to call her "Mom." My mother longed for Marie to call her "Mom" and sulked every time Marie would call her Hazel. Why would Marie want to "bond" with my mother—who spied on her and made her boyfriend/husband miserable?

- *One-sided relationship*: Are you your mom's emotional or spousal surrogate? Does her mental and emotional state depend on her perception of the quality of your relationship with her?

  Does your mental and emotional state depend on the same? Do you feel trapped into a relationship with Mom? Does your relationship with your mom interfere with your life plans such as making and nurturing friends, doing hobbies and activities, parenting, and doing self-care? How? Why?

  It took serious counseling to help me understand how my mother had recruited me to be her emotional surrogate. I listened obediently; my father cheated. I was the youngest and always around; my father wasn't. When my father died, the only emotion my mother expressed to me was that he really didn't love her the way she wanted him to and that she had to take care of him during his sickly periods that led to his death. Is that grief? I now know I can't define anyone else's grief. But, was that information necessary for my ears? My mother needed friends in which to confide, and even counselors brave enough to tell her the truth, but she manipulated them so hard with her martyr-hero syndrome that no one could ever get close enough without her lies and manipulations.

Six months before she died I arranged for her to visit my son in Nashville so she could personally tell him her news of the terminal diagnosis. She began by saying, "Now, Matthew, you know you are my most sensitive and loving grandchild. I want you to make sure you keep that up because I'd like to think you got that from your dad, and he definitely got that from me." I stayed out of the conversation. Afterwards, my son asked me, "Dad, does she really think she helped you to be sensitive? Because you will always be working on your anger issues. Ha! And, what am I supposed to do with the information that I'm the MOST sensitive and emotionally mature grandchild? Does she do this with all the other cousins?" Sadly, I had no response for him.

More Toxic Traits: Shame, Blame, Name, and Maim

Toxic traits and behaviors transcend every field in the mental health profession. So, as you read other researchers or practitioners, you will discover repetition and overlap in their diagnosis and treatment of the issues, perhaps with another perspective or context. Remember, *toxicity is one person placing demands (our personal set of rules for the way life should be) on others and then insisting in destructive ways that those demands be met.*

So, like "one-sided relationships" in the above list, a toxic mother believes life will be better when you show her your appreciation or obey her will. She simply singles you out to bring her the life she believes she deserves.

Other professionally and universally accepted toxic traits exist in mothers that reflect my definition of toxicity. The literature is replete with examples, descriptions, ways to identify the traits, and ways to heal from them. In each case, we can see how it is not just the trait itself, but the way in which the toxic mother demands others comply with her RTLB. Consolidating most toxic behaviors to four easily identifiable actions or reactions helps those who struggle to self-reflect or who do not feel free admitting their feelings. So most toxic behaviors fall into one of four categories: Toxic mothers shame, blame, name and maim.

They will shame you in both subtle and egregious ways only they can know. They can push your buttons because they helped create those buttons. They will place blame on you to deflect their own negligence, culpability, or abuse. They can name your most humiliating experiences publicly or to you individually, bringing them up at the most opportune time—simply to knock you off your game. In today's terms, they will "call you out" and expose you as a fraud, a hypocrite, an imbecile, a weakling, exposing every weakness they know you have. They will maim your character or your body, insulting you conveniently to keep you on the defensive or bring you to your knees with any kind of oppression they can conjure—physical, mental, spiritual, emotional, overt, or covert. So, when you feel ashamed, guilty, vulnerable, or beaten, let those feelings be the impetus for you to seek healing, personal responsibility, and power in an opportunity to grow into the man of virtue and integrity you wish to become. There is a lot of help out there.

Illustrations From My Life: Hope Is Out There!

In front of her friends and mine, my mother would conveniently bring up how messy I kept my house. I knew it was not to kid me, since she had complained so frequently about staying at my wife's and my house to the point of my moving her and my father to a hotel. She knew my friends were aware of my clutter, and she knew I was defenseless in front of her friends. Her "life," according to our definition, came when she kept control of me through shame, blame, name, and maim. I was embarrassed to admit how much I hated her badgering and my anger grew consistently as she brought up my clutter in the most opportune times for her to drive home yet another time that I could not match her cleanliness, that I had ignored her "motherly" training, that I had no respect for her or my friends by having so much clutter around. You get the point. I needed a way out.

My mother took this to the next level when she needed to control whether we thought she favored us, whether she saw us as acceptable. She did so by creating false images and a false sense of security while gossiping about someone else. My mother chose this approach to moralize. We were constantly trying to guess what and who mattered to her and why. She badgered my brother not to live with his girlfriend and not to drink, yet she allowed her daughter to live and sleep with a very useless, drug-addicted man. And she preyed on my confusion over the inconsistency in which she intervened with my siblings.

During her last six months of life, my brother and I would compare our stories and conversations with our mom. On every topic, Mom was pitting us against each other, telling him one thing that made him suspect me and vice versa. He and I chose not to entertain the shame or blame of not living up to her standards. We refused to manipulate back at her but instead to confront the truth of her comparison game when we discovered any inconsistency or plot.

In the last ten years of my sister's life, my sister and I discovered that my mother would criticize our personal parenting style and tell us individually that the other sibling's style is better than ours. She and I realized neither of our parental styles was perfect, but that it served my mother's best toxic interest to pit us against each other. Lisa and I had no reason to be jealous of the other and every reason to bond over our mutual interest to be the best parents we could be. Mom thought her life was better when I was off my game, doubting whether my parental style was appropriate and acceptable to her. She believed I would run to her for validation and love. I automatically assumed her praise for my sister's style was a condemnation of mine, which was her ultimate goal. She would name—label—me as arrogant or elitist simply because I chose to travel the country and the world with my wife and children and not be a homebody catering to her every whim—something to which my sister had unfortunately fallen prey.

You can't turn on the radio or television today without hearing the word "gaslighting," another toxic trait that moms and politicians alike perfect in their inappropriate search for control and life. Interestingly, I struggled when my mother would gaslight, but I, too, gaslight other people. Gaslighting is domestic abuse where the gaslighter uses whatever tactic to get the survivor to doubt his sanity, self-esteem, and much more. Mom's modus operandi to gaslight? Shaming, blaming, naming, or maiming. She might deny ever saying or doing something abusive when brought to her attention. She might accuse her victims that they are overreacting to one of her inappropriate behaviors. She might make fun of your weaknesses to your wife knowing it will make you fume. The goal of a gaslighter is to detract from the fact that she is abusing her victims.[13] When moms gaslight, they confuse their children, who naturally obey authority. Then, as adults, the children can't trust their emotions, their sanity, or their perceptions.

As will be told in greater detail later in this book, my mother knowingly placed my infant son in a dangerous and vulnerable position when he was three months old. I only found out she purposely did it when my son was six. When I discovered the truth, I hung up, gathered my thoughts, and called my mother back. I calmly told her I would never be taking my family to Pennsylvania again, but that my parents were welcome in my home whenever they chose. She asked why and I replied that my duty as a father is to protect my son and I couldn't trust her anymore. Her response? "Guy, I thought you were a Christian. So much for forgive and forget! Your religion doesn't mean $hit!" It was a complete non sequitur for me, but I still held my ground. She wanted to gaslight, shaming me for the hypocrisy of my faith and avoid the need for serious apology and self-reflection. But, I put the fire out by walking away and staying true to the values and virtues that I believed superseded any of her abuse.

When toxic mothers shame, blame, name, and maim, they are trying to avoid the responsibility for severing the trusting relationship with their sons and ignoring the collateral damage of insisting their RTLB are followed. These behaviors rob their victim of a sense of belonging, and men especially find it easy to substitute less-than-perfect, unfulfilling community that insulates and isolates: drinking buddies, pornography, extramarital affairs, and more. (We'll discuss this in Chapter 8.) With such emotional frustration from the gaslighting, men often feel as though their mother will never own her collateral damage or destructive behaviors, always setting up someone else to blame, including you. This strips sons of hope or healing.

Finally, shaming, blaming, naming, and maiming are much more effective when toxic mothers withhold the truth from their sons. They guard the truth and perpetuate lies, only revealing as much as is needed to keep their sons guessing when Mom will loosen her control on their psyches.

For example, Mom constantly told me that my children were going to have terrible lives because they grew up in more affluent circumstances than either my parents' or my siblings' families. Even though I was overly generous with my resources to my parents, my mother constantly told me I was selfish and that my siblings were more generous with their time and resources than I. This marginalizing left me wondering if something was wrong with me and the way I was parenting and loving my wife simply because my mother never included me in her inner sanctum consisting of my sister's and brother's families. I doubted myself and my own sonship.

My mother became engaged to another man, Roy, two years after my father passed away. She constantly told me he didn't want to get married. She would tell me he was anti-social. She would lament that he didn't have any friends and that she had to drag him to social things. But, even now, years after his death and my mother's, too, I receive conflicting reports. I'll never know who did not want to get married and who wanted to "live in sin" (my mother's words). My mother was constantly controlling the spin on her truth. Remember Hazel World? What is the truth and what is the lie and why can't she just tell me straight? Mom got to blame others and name her facts to put the best manipulative spin possible on simple living.

Some of Roy's friends, who are now my friends, told me he had an abundance of friends and athletic hobbies that my mother stifled with her gate keeping, grooming him to be her little puppet. She was maiming his reputation and his social life. She constantly used him as the excuse—a scapegoat—when Roy would complain that he, Mom, and I were going to another social function. "Roy needs to get out more," she would tell me in front of him, shaming us both into submission. She consistently attempted to convince me that he was bringing her down. I believe they both were consensual adults in the scapegoating department. It was simply convenient for my mother to use Roy as the scapegoat for her guilt and immaturity in handling her cohabitation and his to hold on to his wealth for his children while maintaining the intense structured routine he craved with predictable friends: pickleball/tennis buddies, hunting buddies, medical marijuana support groups. The two of them insulated and isolated themselves as individuals. My mother manipulated their outside world to be the gate keeper for their relationship as a couple.

My mother regularly withheld truth from me in order to drop her own version of facts and fantasy into her manipulative shenanigans. I experienced the oppression from her stonewalling, as it left me unable to make legitimate life decisions in relation to her. Is she really sick? Will she follow through with her prescribed medications? If I tell her how I feel, will she withdraw her affection from me and my family?

Even though I was sacrificing weeks out of my life to handle Roy's sickness, his death, my mother's blindness, and her terminal illness—all a continent and a day's travel away—she made me second-guess the facts and truth regarding her circumstances so I would dote all over her. I asked her if she was sick over and over and she lied that everything was terrific, but she kept dropping hints that it might not be. It made me badger her for the truth, but she waited a month to tell me her doctor had found metastatic cancer and that she had refused treatment. She called it "privacy." I call it stonewalling.

The results? Lost time with my mother, anxiety over wondering whether she was hiding something, a completely frenzied and unpredictable personal schedule, and my failed attempts at trying to love and serve my mother well. How can a man grow in virtue and integrity when his efforts are thwarted at every corner? As toxic mothers shame, blame, name, and maim, sons internalize their pain, continuing the cycle. They create their own rules-to-live-by while insulating or isolating themselves from any healthy support that might help them out of their mother's black hole.

Back to Our Definition

Remember, toxicity is one person placing demands on others and then insisting in destructive ways that those demands be met. We are all capable of being the perpetrator. We are all capable of healing our own self-inflicted wounds as much as we are our mother-inflicted ones.

This broad definition of "toxic" captures the essence of every one of these traits and behaviors in its two words: *demands* and *insisting*. If we are able to identify what sorts of beliefs and demands we have created for our own life as well as the demands our mothers place on us, we are well on our way to designing creative and personal approaches to healing and becoming less toxic ourselves. The next chapter helps you simplify and clarify toxic behaviors and call them what they are. The demands on others and the insistence that others comply are simply rules that the offending mother believes will validate the life she feels she deserves.

I hope you find the analogy as helpful as I do even now, years after my mother's death.

CHAPTER 4

CREATING TOXICITY OR DESIGNING HEALING? THAT IS THE QUESTION

How do we begin to heal our lives so we respond differently to our toxic mothers? We all develop and internalize *rules for life* and we impose those rules onto others even though we, ourselves, cannot abide by the same rules. At times, we don't even hold ourselves accountable to our own rules. So, when and how do we become toxic ourselves? And how did our mothers become toxic? If we initiate our change by examining these "rules," then we can reverse the process to detoxify and create a custom healing plan that relates directly to our lives with our toxic moms. What is the nature of these rules? I call them *rules-to-live-by*.

Rules-to-live-by (RTLB) are a description or prescription of how we want the world and others to function. Rules-to-live-by are what **we believe will bring us "life" however we define life.** Fill in the blanks: My life will be better if/when_____. If only _____, then things will work out in my favor. For example, "My life will be better when I get a raise/promotion/divorce, etc." Or, "If my mother would only see that I'm doing what I love, then she wouldn't be on my case so much." We all entertain these thoughts, but sons and mothers alike have crossed the lines when they demand their conditions be met, especially when those demands or conditions hurt someone, even ourselves. We'll examine how these rules are generated soon, but for now consider this illustration.

Yes, Mother!

We easily allow a simple life experience to evolve into a life-giving rule for us and, as an extension, for others to follow. These rules then become part of our lifestyle, habits, or expectations. As the rules-to-live-by are validated by others around us, we even cluster these rules into larger contexts such as politeness or wokeness or any other cultural norm. Simply by living, we impose our rules onto others and/or we adopt other people's.

As a young son, I innocently received the input of my toxic mother without questioning the validity or safety of doing so. I grew up with my mother forcing me to call her "Mother" instead of "Mom" with serious consequences for calling her the latter instead of the former. She physically hit me or grounded me unrealistically when I responded to her by shouting back instead of coming at her beck and call. If I did not physically march to her presence like a dog to his dinner bowl but instead returned her shout with "What?" or "Just a minute," I suffered the same extreme punishments she used for "improper title address."

As I grew up, I formed a cluster of rules-to-live-by one rule at a time. The way to show respect to my mother is to do what she wants and never to question her intentions or legitimacy in making such requests. Then, in reaction to her rules, I formed a personal cluster of RTLB. My mother simply wanted me to show her respect, but I was responsible for reading her mind when she chose to enforce it. I paid the price if I interpreted the rule's application wrong.

After internalizing this rule, years later I began reflecting on why I had such rage when my own children dismissed me or my expectations for them. I would flip out if my students or employees challenged my directives. I was now imposing my mother's same rule-to-live-by onto my children and others. My mother derived life out of controlling us under the disguise of "showing her respect." I'm responsible for how I've internalized those RTLB and created my own toxicity. Some clinicians call this internalization part of the mother wound.[14]

Creating Toxicity

The figure that follows describes the overall process for how we all create toxicity. Some of us allow ourselves to develop toxic behaviors unconsciously, others feed on anger, bitterness, and fear to fuel the process, but still others end up happy, reversing this process whether they are aware of it or not. Either way, we as sons add our unique touches to the process. Consider each component of Figure 1.

There are three areas of life decisions that men consciously or unconsciously develop and internalize, all of which leave the son vulnerable and disposed to deriving his own set of toxic RTLB. First, in reaction to their toxic mothers and external demands, men at times make extensive choices to *reject* their former life and/or deny their conscience. They might turn their back completely on their mother or choose to live carpe diem, without a care or moral compass regarding anything, especially their mother. Second, men *escape* impulsively at times looking for something else (sometimes unhealthy such as pornography, womanizing, machismo) to replace or reduce the complexity of having to submit to their toxic mother. The ultimate goal of escaping and replacing is to provide themselves with the instant gratification they believe will deliver them from the emptiness or frustration of relating to their toxic mother. My impulsive escape included pouring myself into higher education to the point of becoming intellectually arrogant and self-righteous.

Finally, knowingly or unknowingly, men sometimes *isolate* themselves from the healthy input and support from others or, conversely, they *insulate* themselves with like-minded men or culture. In both cases, they are attempting to validate themselves and their life-choices, especially regarding their reactions to their toxic mothers. Any one of these three reactions to Mom's toxicity leaves the door open for sons to create unhealthy RTLB they, themselves, cannot uphold but which they impose on others along their path, all believing they will find "life," safety, and freedom there. As we blow in the wind without a compass or sail, trying to enforce the rules that we believe will now bring us life, we end up at the beginning of the process *again*, rejecting outside virtues and values, impulsively escaping the next toxic environments, and isolating or insulating ourselves from healthy input.

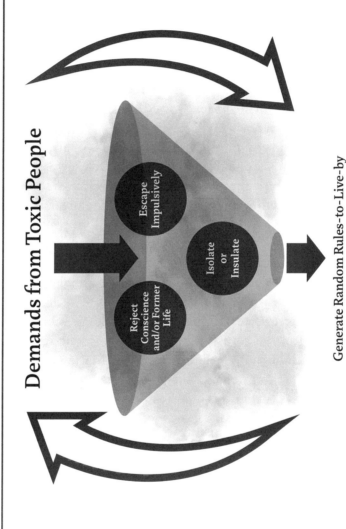

BECOMING TOXIC

Demands from Toxic People

Escape Impulsively

Isolate or Insulate

Reject Conscience and/or Former Life

Generate Random Rules-to-Live-by

Figure 1: Becoming Toxic

Living in Hazel World

My mother's toxic world was a prison to which only she held the key. I named that world in her honor: Hazel World. As a child I had no choice but swallow Mom's toxic poison and live there. After escaping from Hazel World at nineteen years old and rejecting every way of life that ever occurred in Hazel World, my mother still continually told me how inferior and flawed I was because, at twenty years old, I married into a family wealthier and more educated or more concerned with social graces than my parents. Even though I never lived in the same town when I left, I lived confused in Hazel World until my daughter was born.

Mom would erupt like Old Faithful and broadly spewed her toxicity as much as she could over my attempts to grow up. For example, she constantly brought to my attention her RTLB that because of my resources, I certainly could *not* have a meaningful life or relationship. She would ask questions like, "Is going to Europe more important than seeing your family in Pennsylvania?" And, she insisted I was judging them for their intelligence since I have a PhD and they only a high school diploma. I couldn't win and not a single aspect of my life away from Lancaster escaped her scrutinous tentacles.

According to her "Hazel World" thinking, she accused me of being embarrassed to associate with them. I was robbing them of their grandchildren even though my wife (Marie) and I consistently invited them to our home whenever they wanted for as long as they wanted. She criticized our home calling it a "materialistic hoarder's nightmare." In my presence, she would tell her friends how superficial and meaningless my life was since all I did was hang with academics and travel the world. She insulated herself with people who just nodded their heads in agreement, scared she would sink her venomous teeth into their necks. She would call us selfish even though we paid for their house to be remodeled any way they wanted, threw them a fiftieth anniversary and two retirement parties, paid for my niece's wedding, helped my brother and his middle son with both their home mortgages, fixed my parents' house deck and foundation when termites destroyed it, bought them a car, and much more.

I'm not trying to brag here. I'm trying to make sense of a world where someone would accuse their own child of something for which there is CONTRARY evidence. Both my immediate family and my family of origin regularly suffered at the hand of the negative, toxic ruler of Hazel World, but we continued to return to that world hoping for different results.

The judgment and oppression coming from this "frail" and sweet lady with "no enemies" was ever-present. And, for all intents and purposes, my brother and I raised ourselves from my age twelve. My sister's physical and mental health issues annexed my parents' attention, so the abuses towards us simply became more efficient. Almost ritualistically, when our mother would lasso our two lives into her deranged sense of reality, we would simply glance at each other and mouth the words, "Hazel World."

This was our signal that we both see the lunacy and the truth and that we acknowledge the danger of challenging the former with the latter. This stark and suffocating insanity blinded me of alternative ways I might respond to being in Hazel World. I was also relying on my own self-made RTLB. Instead of reflecting on a mature, loving approach to my mother's sulfur, I simply blamed her for the misery in which my brother and I found ourselves.

By the age of twenty-five, my impulse to reject my mother's legitimate pain and suffering while she dealt with my sister led me to justify my own selfish and vindictive thoughts, acts, and rules without considering the consequences of my actions toward her or anyone. I had no compassion in me to understand her perspective so that anything she did would be filtered through my anger. Whether toxic or not, my rules-to-live-by did not allow me to see anything but toxicity. Blame was the name of my game.

This lack of conscience kept me from seeing that I was treating my wife and my children with the same rigid demand for conformity. I couldn't see that I was a narcissistic king demanding the worship of others in a world they were coming to hate as much as I hated Hazel World. I had generated enough of my own RTLB that I bundled into toxic weapons for those who would cross my invisible, unspoken, and inappropriate boundaries in Guy World. It took a few "rock-bottom" events to push me to begin the healing process and even choose to reenter that Hazel World with the goal of loving, respecting, comforting, and honoring my mother during her last six months of life. How did I heal myself? How did I free myself to become a better version of myself where I am not oppressed by others' RTLB, nor do I oppress and retaliate?

Designing a Path Toward Healing

Let's reverse engineer the process represented in Figure 1. There is as much support and research to help sons heal from the effects of their toxic mothers as there is to describe how mothers are toxic.[15] Figure 2 that follows consolidates all the research so we can customize our healing process to fit our needs and circumstances. In order to heal, a son must first assume responsibility for his own toxicity. This means evaluating the quality and nature of your relationships, including with your mother. This, by definition, will inevitably lead you to examine your own RTLB that you push onto others. Remember, your RTLB are only toxic when you demand others follow them, inappropriately or immaturely insisting they meet your needs and bring you "life." How are your rules toxic to others? How did you develop those rules for life?

After reflecting on the motives behind your RTLB, it is time for you to develop your own identity. In doing so, you will need to generate *new* RTLB that define the kind of man and son you want to be. What bigger picture goals and ambitions would you like to accomplish? On what virtues would you like to design yourself? What kind of RTLB can help you achieve those goals to change your habits and character into something you can respect? Once you've established a clear set of RTLB, try them out in the real world. *Enjoy* freedom from imprisonment—guilt-free! *Seek* the help you need with humility, focus, and determination. And with Grace and Truth, never stop working on yourself to reclaim your integrity and become a loving, compassionate, safe person unafraid to love and be loved. If you understand the healing process according to Figure 2, then you can easily assimilate and internalize the amazing advice out there for us who want to heal.

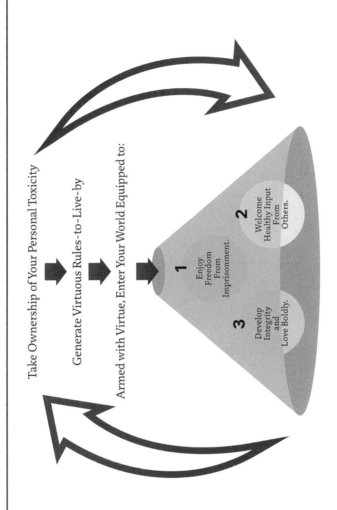

HEALING ON YOUR OWN TERMS

Take Ownership of Your Personal Toxicity

Generate Virtuous Rules-to-Live-by

Armed with Virtue, Enter Your World Equipped to:

1 Enjoy Freedom From Imprisonment.

2 Welcome Healthy Input From Others.

3 Develop Integrity and Love Boldly.

Figure 2: Healing On Your Own Terms

SECTION 2

Breaking Down the Healing Process

CHAPTER 5

TAKE OWNERSHIP OF YOUR PERSONAL TOXICITY

First Steps First

The first step in the healing process encourages wounded sons to take ownership of our personal toxicity.[16] To do that, we must first accept the idea that in reacting to our toxic mother's RTLB, we placed ourselves on a path that perhaps left us toxic as well. We must acknowledge her rules-to-live-by and begin our own transformation and healing by looking at the origins of her desperate rules to hang on to a life over which she has little or no control. You will learn my mother's story in Chapter 6. But, you must also acknowledge your own RTLB and their effect on the people you love.

Now that you are an adult, you can choose whose rules to follow, which rules to follow, the results you would like to see by you or others following those rules, and so much more. You begin taking responsibility by first looking at the quality of your relationships with others and your purpose for being in such relationships. Your honesty and humility will lead you straight to your own RTLB. Some may be healthy, some may be neutral, and some may be toxic. It is your responsibility to identify the origin of your toxic demands, and the only way to find out which ones are toxic is to examine how you have hurt others, especially those whom you love.

An Honest Look

For example, I was bickering with my wife, and my daughter, Hope, butted in. Hope had an opinion that happened to strengthen Marie's argument. I raged at her so violently she is still afraid to speak up sometimes, even when I ask for her input. I had obviously damaged her psyche at my own expense. I had to ask myself where all that came from. I had to ask why? What was the rule-to-live-by that triggered me to be so toxic? What did I think was so life-giving that I would break down my ability to speak into her life with hope, love, and encouragement? I had to look inward to begin to control the outward.

As a child, during a family squabble, my mother would slap us if we came to the defense of one of our siblings whom she was disciplining. She was the authority, and we had no rights or due process. After the slap, if we spoke up again with an opinion or with a fact that might exonerate our brother or sister, she would ground BOTH of us for colluding. Her rule-to-live-by was "No one challenges me, and if they do, they are disrespecting me. Respect is only given by admitting I am right." Another of her rules was, "My punishments are for their own good. They are learning who's in charge, whom to respect, how to get along in the real world."[17] Remember, it became toxic when she forced those rules onto us in inappropriate and hurtful ways.

When I realized I was wrong with my daughter, I apologized, but I also went down a path to discover what I was after. My rule-to-live-by was different than my mother's, but it was toxic all the same. From reacting to my mother's craziness, I decided that "fairness" was life. It's not fair that I couldn't "save" my brother or sister with my piece of wisdom and insight. It's not fair that Mom always assumed she was right. Life is better when things are fair, and I believed I had my finger on the pulse of what is fair or not. I was the fairness god, and I demanded that others idolize me for it.

My wife is a strong woman and an even stronger debater. She thinks quickly and broadly, but she is always relevant. I, on the other hand, process things emotionally first. For me, having a discussion with my wife almost always requires a second discussion, but we each offer the other grace and forgiveness. She blurts out her opinions right away, and I need to sift through my numb reaction to any assertiveness, raging internally that assertiveness is not "fair." When my daughter interrupted with damaging evidence, I only saw two-on-one. Not fair, especially because I was obviously in the wrong already, and I wanted to win the argument at any expense! That one rule-to-live-by made me impose hurtful rules onto my daughter and wife that they didn't deserve. The rule made me insist that our daughter read my mind and know she was not welcome. I needed to own the fact that my rule to be fair was not fair at all—it was harmful and toxic.

I needed to create a new rule to keep me from hurting her again. You will practice creating your own rules in later chapters, but for now simply know I created these new rules: Loving my family is more important than me being right about something petty. I'm going to keep my overinflated sense of fairness in check and perhaps even deescalate my rage by asking for input from others I respect and people I trust or that are close to the situation. I'm going to stop when I'm raging and ask what is so important. Then, I will ask myself, "Is this more important than your family's health and well-being?" Encouraging dialogue will now bring me a new life instead of demanding others acquiesce, and I can be more intentional about how I love and respect those I cherish.

Taking Charge: What the Experts Say

There are lots of sources that provide help for us to reflect on our own role in a difficult and toxic exchange with our mothers. Karen Young's website, Hey Sigmund, compiles a vast amount of research and makes it accessible to her followers.[18] Her blog, *Stronger for the Breaks—How to Heal from a Toxic Parent*, states the first step of Figure 2: "Be careful of your own toxic behaviour." Her advice is well detailed regarding how to assume responsibility for our own toxicity and healing. She encourages us to weigh the costs of letting go of the relationship with our mother altogether or returning to her, but she does it by giving us permission—freedom—to do it without listening to the negative toxicity that our mothers hurl at us or that we might be telling ourselves.

Young believes it is important to know and define exactly what we want "love" to look like . . . both the way our mother loves us individually and the way we wish to love others including Mom. She opens the door for us to close the door when and if we are not being loved and respected. We will make mistakes, especially ones that will trigger our negative self-talk or that hurt others but, worse, that will provide ammunition for our toxic mothers to beat us back into submitting to her RTLB. We can and will make mistakes, but our worst-case scenario is that we work to heal ourselves by trial and error *without* our mothers. We must be willing to accept that.

Essentially, our RTLB grow out of our beliefs about how the world works or should work. Those beliefs can be assumptions about ourselves, self-talk, self-protection from the hurt and dysfunction of our past, or anything. So, the key is to figure out what beliefs get in your way and stop you from doing what you want to do, saying what you want to say, or being who you want to be. Were you brought up to believe your opinion doesn't count? That parents are always right? That you're unlovable? Unimportant? Stupid? Annoying? Incapable? Worthless? Has it cost you relationships? Happiness? Freedom to be? To experiment? To explore?[19]

Should or Shouldn't?

Whether you can or can't form a relationship with your mother, whether you want to or not, the research on healing from toxic mothers suggests you form a family or support groups of your own. This family can consist of anyone you wish, such as a family of friends that you know safely love you well and who are mature enough for you to be yourself in trying to love them. This is what a family is and does and should be. Without intentional work to *find focus with friendship* (discussed in Chapter 8), a toxic mother will sabotage your ability to experiment with your own RTLB and keep you from developing into a man of integrity and virtue. These rules-to-live-by, according to Young and many other researchers, are not a list of do's and don'ts, but without intentional reflection such as that recommended in this book, our lives devolve into attempts to obey an unrealistic and unattainable set of laws dictating what we should or should not do to validate our existence to people who may or may not be our advocate.

Young suggests we find our "'shoulds' that shouldn't be." Young's "shoulds" are rules-to-live-by. She points out that some are good, such as "I should be around people who respect me." But some RTLB are bad. "I should always be nice." Once we've clarified the beliefs that have fueled the toxic RTLB affecting us—ours or Mom's—then we must take proactive steps to enter our life in ways that help us grow into and sustain a healthier and more loving and virtuous life. When you assume responsibility for your own toxicity you will be confronted by the RTLB you've allowed to dominate your life. You might even leave everyday events and interactions with a sense that "I should have done X or Y," shaming and blaming yourself unnecessarily. Your goal, then, is to generate healthy rules that lay the groundwork for you to design a life of freedom with the tools to love others and yourself boldly, all while maintaining your integrity and self-respect.

Grab Hold of Your Life!

Brianna Wiest, author of multiple books on self-healing, self-sabotage, and self-care, wrote the most succinct acknowledgment of our need to begin healing. The title of her blog post from the website Thought Catalog says it all: What Happened To You Was Not Your Fault, But How You Go Forward Is Your Responsibility.[20]

> Life hurts us all in different ways, but it is how we respond—and who we become—that determines whether a trauma becomes a tragedy, or the beginning of the story of how the victim became the hero. (April 2021).

Wiest encourages us to take responsibility for our own healing. She believes we can embrace our healing "as a gift." Avoiding our need to heal will make us "dependent and bitter." She encourages us to take charge of our "unprocessed pain" so we can love well those important to us.

> Healing is our responsibility because "healing" is actually not returning to how and who we were before,

it is becoming someone we have never been—someone stronger, someone wiser, someone kinder.

When we heal, we step into the people we have always wanted to be. We are not only able to metabolize the pain, we are able to affect real change in our lives, in our families, and in our communities. We are able to pursue our dreams more freely. We are able to handle whatever life throws at us, because we are self-efficient and assured. We are more willing to dare, risk, and dream of broader horizons, ones we never thought we'd reach.

You Mean, I Get to Choose?

As a survivor of a toxic mother, I found it almost foreign that I could dream about the kind of human being I wanted to be. How does one move on? My mother's bindings and my youthful pride and anger made me so reactionary, I never understood how to be proactive in designing myself, at least until it was almost too late, too ingrained in my soul that I was unworthy, unable, unlovable, powerless, and more. Early on in my therapy, I recall being asked if I had any role models of men who treated me like I wanted to be treated, like I wanted to treat others, and who practiced the kind of character I wanted for myself. At first, I said no. I was numb to the idea of looking up to people who had influenced my life. My therapist gave me the same encouragement as Wiest. *It is up to me to decide how I want to be and to quit waiting around for my pain to subside, for my life to get better, for someone to rescue me.* Instead of dwelling on my mother's paralyzing, toxic projections, I can look into my own heart to find the ways I want to love and live. I can even look at other people's healthy RTLB and adapt them for myself. Here's one such example.

A Tribute to Jack Brunner

This is a sentimental shoutout to Jack Brunner, the owner of the private gymnastics gym in which I practiced while I was in high school. Jack knew a lot about sports and gymnastics, but he wasn't my coach. He let Jim Tarnowski and John Lideen do that. Instead, he coached the elite females. Even at the age of fourteen, I immediately noticed three things about Jack. First, he loved his wife. He affirmed her. He made her laugh. And, even though she did not appear athletic and he was a college football player, he welcomed her to be an integral part of his team . . . of THEIR team. Together, they constructed their harmonious and happy life. Second, he rarely raised his voice, and, when he did, it was not yelling or abusive. I didn't know that was possible. Third, he was confident in who he was, and he sported a really cool leather chauffeur cap to prove it.

I worked for Jack in three capacities just to pay my dues to be on the club team, and I'm pretty sure he knew how directionless, unformed, and lacking in parental support I was. While I was feeling irrelevant and unworthy, Jack welcomed me. He boldly lived his life with character, showing me his purpose-driven life of joy, confidence, trust, and inclusivity. His rules-to-live-by were to love, respect, empower others, and so much more.

I wanted that from him and others. And, I wanted to live by those same rules for and toward others, affecting others just as positively with my own character and compassion. What did I do in my naïve and desperate longing to be like him? I saved my money and had custom-made a suede cap exactly like his (I couldn't afford leather), and I wore it everywhere I could. I loved that hat. It defined me. It gave me hope. It gave me confidence. It reminded me of Jack's RTLB. It reminded me to be kind, to give others the benefit of the doubt, to encourage others instead of being in despair over my own life. Guess what I did with that hat? After less than a year, I traded it with my sister for a nickel bag of weed!

If I can recall this role model from the age of fourteen and articulate someone else's healthy RTLB, then we men can certainly look to each other and decide for ourselves individually and collectively what kind of character we want to have.

Me? Toxic?

In therapy, I had to own my anger outbursts that hurt my wife. I had to admit I wasn't going to be that perfect parent I thought I would be simply because I was free from my mother's tentacles. I demanded others believe what I projected about myself, even if it wasn't true. Of course, my heart was full of anger that no one could read my mind or know my pain and certainly no one validated that I was as "terrific" as I wanted to think of myself. I found my identity in being helpful, smart, insightful, generous, and more, but it didn't fulfill me. Others didn't and couldn't know how desperately I wanted to be loved, and I wasn't telling them. I couldn't see I was depending on outside influences to validate me. It was my prideful "right" that they comply with my RTLB and give me the life I deserved. I was sad; I brought others into my mess. I was lonely even though I "helped" so many. I was becoming passive-aggressive.

Maybe it should have been a red flag when Marie and I moved into our first apartment. I know people talk about the toilet seat phenomenon. I had that down (the seat, that is). I was compliant. I "obeyed" Marie's wishes. But, my first display of rage and toxicity came when she came over to "help" me load the dishwasher, a month after we were married. She rinsed a glass and put it in the front of the top rack. *Everybody* knows you load the top rack from the back to the front and push it in as you fill. She couldn't have cared less. She stared at me and placed a second glass in the front, and then a third. I used some expletives, slammed the dishwasher closed, breaking the glasses in the front and said, "YOU do it then!"

Nowhere on my radar was the idea that my rule-to-live-by was, "You may NOT challenge the way I choose to help! In doing so, you are telling me that I am worthless, so worthless that I couldn't even figure out the best way to help." (I think you can probably guess where that came from.) In the ten years after that dishwasher incident, my anger, verbal abuse, and other forms of toxicity were left unchecked, festering and infecting my soul, our marriage, my wife, and so much more. Now you understand why three miscarriages and the threat of early-onset menopause brought us into the marriage counselor.

We need to own our personal toxicity and work on it before we learn to heal from our mother's.

Just Fix It!

When you work on your own toxicity, you will soon discover the best way to identify it is to assess honestly how well you love or how much you hurt others. This process must never end, as our lives and relationships change so much over time. The cycle must continue. And, since lots of men like to find permanent solutions to relational problems, a one-time fix, we become discouraged when our solution to having injured one person does not work on another person or in another context. Part of owning our toxicity is to mature our understanding of relationships and our roles in them.

Two things occur if we avoid examining our hearts and our relational skills simply because we believe we "fixed" this problem or that. We either forget to apply our "fix" to the next scenario and end up hurting someone else or our solution to what we perceive to be the "same problem" doesn't work on different people, and we hurt them with our resentment that they have not followed our rule-solution properly and acquiesced.

In marriage counseling, I learned that my sarcasm was hurting Marie. She would be the brunt of my jokes. I tried to fix it by turning the subject of the joke onto me. I would self-deprecate, and it would be funny to most without hurting her. It worked for a while. But as our lives got busier, I forgot about my commitment to protecting Marie's feelings, especially in public. And, when I returned to my sarcasm, it was more like public shame or blame, not humor. I was too busy to look at my own cruelty in the picture.

A very close friend asked me if I actually believed the self-deprecation I so readily proclaimed. He said it made him feel uncomfortable that I didn't like myself that much. He was right. Then, as our daughter matured more and more, I had forgotten the fix yet again. I realized that in response to both my children's opinions on any subject, my sarcasm expressed to them my disappointment in their character, ideas, or accomplishments. The sadness has made me rethink my solution to my sarcastic attitude in general. Perhaps it comes from a disdain from anything scripted for me. My life was so limited as a young boy that I now resent anything that smacks of authority or limitation of freedoms. I'm now working on that in my counseling. I cannot hurt others consistently and dismiss it as my sense of humor.

The Cycle Continues

We men must never stop taking ownership for hurting others in our lives. This includes assuming responsibility for restoring those we've hurt to a better relationship with themselves, with us, with others or with God (discussed in detail in Chapter 7). The next two chapters describe the next step in the process of healing: Generate Virtuous Rules-to-Live-by. Instead of quick fixes to your mistakes, establishing these sorts of rules will help you create long-term lifestyle changes in yourself that help you love instead of hate, build up instead of tear down, and help instead of hurt. As you discover how to create better RTLB, remember that whatever RTLB you make, the goal is FIRST to love those around you.

You are in charge of how you want to grow and heal with integrity and love. We must know the difference between virtuous and toxic if we are to design RTLB that promote love, kindness, and other virtues like forgiveness. And, as we practice these RTLB on others, we must not underestimate how awkward and gradual the growth process is.

You must practice these rules on those more forgiving before you consider specific rules to love your toxic mother. As you generate new, more virtuous RTLB, you will be able to step out into any aspect of your world to practice and enjoy your newfound freedom, welcome new, healthier input into your life, and love others as best you can. BUT . . . as you do, it is imperative to keep a check on your own toxicity, which will bear its ugly teeth as you enter unfamiliar territories and encounter new or difficult relationships.

There is no shame but rather great integrity in discovering that perhaps one or more of your RTLB has led you to be toxic toward those you are attempting to love. It is your personal responsibility, though, to take yourself back to the beginning of the process to learn how better to love those you are targeting.[21]

CHAPTER 6

IDENTIFYING TOXIC LIFESTYLE RULES-TO-LIVE-BY

Good, Bad, Aware, and Unaware!

Both sons and toxic mothers have established a well-developed personal set of rules-to-live-by. For sons to find healing, we must assess whether those RTLB are good or bad, healthy or toxic, for us to change our lives or to protect the health of the life we truly want to live. But, we formed many of our RTLB at a time when we were unaware of their existence. For any number of reasons, in our youth we missed seeing how our rules and our mother's rules interacted in a way that brought us to this toxic crossroads. We are either aware or unaware of the RTLB affecting our lives.

The good news is that we can choose any time to expose those rules—good OR bad—whether we were aware of them already like habits or unaware of them until we reflected and applied the strategies, sources, and approaches suggested in this book The key is to purge the toxic rules and their effects while bringing healthy rules to the front lines of finding health and healing, either by reinstituting healthy, wholesome RLTB we've suppressed or by creating new RTLB from safe and reliable sources and environments.

We can also consider how these rules add to our virtue or delete from it. In a safe, uncharged environment, we can imagine the man we want to be. This awareness helps you funnel your healing strategies with focus. As you practice your own new sets of RTLB, your actions and reactions begin to fall into place. You experience freedom from the imprisonment of your toxic mother. Your search for healthy input becomes a lifestyle where you enjoy friends, fellowship, and fun. You humbly seek the guidance of professionals and confidants who have your best interests at heart.

You choose to reflect on your life and relationships to help you become aware of and proactive at healing strategies. You can now exercise compassion toward anyone you choose without losing your soul. Now is the time to examine our coping mechanisms and challenge them, including the very rules-to-live-by that limit our ability to act freely within healthy boundaries of love, generosity, kindness, and common-sense respect for and support of ourselves and others.

Toxic Rules or Toxic Lifestyle?

Humility Required

If you are ready to heal from your toxic mother, you must look carefully and humbly at your life's circumstances, admit you need help, and seek help from reliable sources—who may not tell you something you can be proud of. It is up to you to have the integrity to practice virtues and character traits you wish to develop, but you will also need support and discipline to make those kinds of personal changes. To do that you must have two things at the forefront of your identity design process: a clear understanding of the nature of each rule you scrutinize or create and a moral compass that informs you more than simply allowing you to punish your mother, yourself, and others with reactive emotion such as anger and vengeance.

Without this kind of humility, you can discount what you think is a virtue to survive and insulate or isolate yourself. This approach will turn your healing strategy into a vice. Using learned and practiced self-assessment and targeted reflection, healing continues by acknowledging a simple and specific toxic RTLB. This hard work will pay off when you begin to design new RTLB that you know will make you a better person. Then, you can learn to identify clusters of rules that dictate your lifestyle and habits. This will lead you to self-select virtue over vice and begin to step out into a healthier world for you and the ones you choose to love.

Why Reflect?

During her last six months of life, my mother had plenty of time to reflect on her life, but her introspection kept looking for ways to validate the RTLB with which she was so familiar. On her death bed, my mother would repeat over and over again, "All my life, I've been a caregiver. I don't know how to be anything else. I just feel I've never been able to live MY life! It's always living and helping someone else's life." As you read on in this book, you'll be able to piece together only some of the horrors that invaded my toxic mother's youth and beyond.

By the time she was twenty-five years old with a husband and three children, Hazel Arcuri had created volumes of lifestyle RTLB that turned her more and more toxic as she lived. She had internalized these beliefs that follow and more about herself, which resulted in her personal set of RTLB she executed on me in very inappropriate manners. I, in turn, reacted unaware and immaturely, and went on to create my own related toxic sets of RTLB. Whether hers uniquely, mine personally, or RTLB we both shared, my mother and I had both developed toxic ways to enforce the rules when we wanted or needed, no matter the damage we might have caused to the victims on the other end.

Hers, Mine, or Ours—It Doesn't Matter

- You won't amount to anything. Don't even try.

- You must survive and protect those around you and sacrifice your own hopes and dreams. Joy does not accompany life. Duty is your only survival tool.

- You cannot depend on anyone else to protect you, even those who are supposed to or who have promised to. So, you must work hard without showing any vulnerability. And, if people show you mercy or do you a favor, you are totally indebted to them until you balance the scale with your own act or favor. I must decide when the debt is paid in full as much as I get to determine who owes me.

- You must find creative and secret ways to outsmart those who you think are going to hurt you. By default, then, everyone is out to outsmart you, so, you must work harder, faster, and alone.

- You are only valid—and safe—if you are helping those weaker than you . . . weaker for any reason. Again, by default, you must stay away from authority as much as possible and hate those who are stronger than you in any aspect of their life.

- You are OK only if someone needs you. You must demand that other people take advantage of something you have or can do. If they don't communicate their need for you, then you must reject any deeper relationship with them.

- You have no worth outside what others think of you. So, you must always be in control of what others think of you and demand that others communicate such data to you.

- You control others by lying to them, withholding the truth, stretching the truth, or simply telling them what to believe about your reality and theirs. You share and validate only information that projects the pretense of your life. When others challenge that truth, you must put them in their place at any expense.

- You must control what others think of you, so you project a narrative of the life you want everyone to envy, even to the point of believing your own lies . . . withdrawing into your own Hazel World.

- You are superior if you point out other people's flaws and weaknesses, even if you are part of their caregiving or friendship/family community. At all costs, you tell people how they are not independent and how they need you to complete them.

- When helping others, you are free to judge them and their character as you patronize them in the sweetest, most loving way. You can even tell others how weak and needy those you help are, insinuating that you are strong and self-sufficient.

- As long as you are sweet and helpful, no one will question your motives, your morals, your imperfections, or anything. And, if someone challenges that, you will ostracize them like the best of Queen B bullies.

- Now that you're an adult, no one may challenge your understanding of truth and reality, because you must have complete control and power to edit that reality the way you need and deserve. If others take that power away from you, you must find ways to insulate or isolate yourself from them.

- Your instinct to protect others is part of your motherly duty (fatherly, professional, etc.), and no one will take that privilege away. If you insult how I am fulfilling that duty, you will pay.

- If others disagree with you, then they obviously do not love you, and you must prove yourself right and manipulate with your rage and sulking until they acknowledge your version of the truth as valid.

Some of these beliefs I, too, internalized, but others I rejected and substituted something just as shaming or toxic. For example, to this day I am unsure if my helpful attitude is a longing and demand for others to appreciate me. I am afraid someone might expose my mixed bag of motivations and vulnerabilities, so I posture myself as helpful and smart. But, instead of finding creative and secret ways to outsmart those who may hurt me, I instead judge them in my heart as inferior and build a mental case to justify my insensitivity and coldness toward them and their needs. We all must look at how our mothers generated their own toxic RTLB, looking for patterns and clusters that led them to bundle their efforts into a lifestyle of abuse and neglect. But, we must also examine how those same maternal arrows of shame and dysfunction have impaled us in ways that have allowed us to embrace our own lifestyle toxic RTLB. Here's an illustration of how neglecting to reflect on your personal life or RTLB leads you to live a lifestyle where your clusters of RTLB sabotage everyone in your path.

Here's an anecdotal illustration.

I'll Save You

Clint, my mother's father, had no idea he was hurling such sputum into my mom's life. Neither did Oleva, my maternal grandmother. My mother, in attempting solely to survive, had no idea she was internalizing their rules-to-live-by as well as formulating her own out of irrational and juvenile denial of her parents' toxicity, evil, and neglect. Mom fled from her home with a subconscious but reactionary embrace of her parents' RTLB. One of Oleva's was, "Hey, I'm doing the best I can, and I can't change this situation. I'm stuck in this life, and you children will just have to fend for yourselves." What a grandma! Clint's was more evil, something like, "You are my property and I must force you into that inferior role that makes you helpless so I can do whatever I want to make myself feel like the king."

In her attempt to escape, Mom simply chose to adopt different rules she believed would bring her a better life. She did not examine her own RTLB or her own motives or wounds. As she internalized her parents' toxic RTLB, she committed to a new set. I must be there for my siblings and protect them from our evil, selfish, and clueless parents. She was left with fear, anger, bitterness, and even pressure to save those she cared about. The toxicity increased every time she took on a new role: sister, fiancée, wife, mother, grandmother, widow, fiancée again, and terminally ill.

She constantly grieved how all she did was care for others. She would say, "I took care of my siblings. Then I married your dad and I had to take care of him. He didn't know how to do anything. And all he did in return is to go off and have affair upon affair in every town we ever lived. Then, I took care of you kids. I really wanted to be a mother, but your dad just didn't bring in enough money. So, I went out and took a job. I made more than your dad! But, then I had to take care of Lisa." (Lisa had been in a car wreck on her way to outpatient therapy for mental illness and addiction. She was in a coma for eight days and needed intensive rehabilitation for years to come.) My mother would continue: "I went to work, visited the hospital at lunch, went back to work, went back to the hospital, and then went to bed and did it all over again. Just like a robot! Then, I had to raise your sister's kids. And then I had to take care of your father, who just wouldn't take care of his own health. And then I had to take care of Roy" (her fiancé with whom she lived until he passed away from lung cancer).

All my mother's RTLB clustered around her martyrdom. She was living the lifestyle of a martyr, demanding that others appreciate her for saving them. But, when that martyrdom was challenged in any way, her lifestyle RTLB pummeled me, my dreams, my initiative, my creativity, and my sanity.

A Hopeful Deflection

As I entered her world for the last time, my mother's lifestyle rules had softened. The rule that I worship the queen of Hazel World had lost its toxicity. Why? I sensed an ironic softening in my own heart. How could I smile intentionally in the midst of Mother heaping her RTLB guilt onto me in the weakest voice I'd ever heard and the frailest body I'd ever embraced? Why do I *not* just scream "hypocrite" when she insists on my compliance to her rules, and how is she backing down and listening after she asks me for MY truth? What is different? I listened to the same diatribe but instead of reacting in shame, self-defense, and de-escalation mode, in return I asked her to reflect on her own life. Those same guilt-slinging demands for praising her martyrdom inspired me to demonstrate compassion.

She toxically began this last stage of her life by stating how ungrateful my brother and I were for how our parents raised us. She kept saying, "Guy, I was a good mother, right?" I evaded the question. But after demonstrating to her that I could love and care for her with no strings attached and after having healed myself some, instead of feeling trapped to lie and say yes, I simply said, "Tell me what makes you want to ask me that."

I deflected her demand back onto her in a way that helped her see her toxic RTLB. She wanted me to admit that she raised Mark and me "so much better" than her parents raised her. She backed down her toxicity concentration, and I listened for a bigger picture that allowed me to practice the love and compassion for which I would like to be known.

In her world, fathers beat their children and smashed their faces into the puddle of urine released from wetting the bed in complete fear of the drunken maniac father entering their bedroom every night. In that world, the children's mother sits in view of such abuse, watches the scene like the newest TV show in color, or reads magazines while her children become frigid punching bags required to pleasure their dad. This is my maternal grandparents' world.

My mom and dad had decided to raise their kids with "love and tenderness" because neither set of their parents (my father was one of ten siblings, my mother one of six) believed in the physical, emotional, mental, or spiritual well-being of any of their children. My parents believed "love will find a way," but they kept secrets about themselves and their upbringing to the point of denying their children—us—any kind of relationship based on truth. They had substituted their parents' RTLB with another set just as toxic. "Our children will be better and do better because of our parenting." Mom and Dad had simply rejected the demands of their parents and relied on whim to adopt new random and potentially toxic RTLB.

I slowly but consciously forged my way to look at my grandparents', my parents', and my own lifestyles and began to see patterns in the composition of our vice-filled RTLB. These helpful categories do not encompass every rule or every lifestyle pattern, but they do put you in a mindset to reflect on their impacts. The rest of this chapter will focus on toxic lifestyle clusters of rules-to-live-by.[22]

Toxic Lifestyle Clusters of RTLB

1. Read My Mind

Sometimes a rule-to-live-by acts like a value or moral principle people want you to approve. Maybe it's as simple as preaching against or justifying a love of money and prestige. Maybe it is a personal or familial blind commitment to a principle such as, "If Mama ain't happy, ain't nobody happy," or, "Children are seen and not heard," or, "You will not embarrass me, so you'd better do exactly what I say exactly the way I want it done." In each of these scenarios, the judge for whether you have followed the rule appropriately or not lies in the hearts and minds of others, who, by nature of the demands themselves, are probably toxic. We must please someone at their unspoken whim. We must satisfy someone's demands with great fear of disappointment. The locus of control is completely from without, outside our influence and our best interest. Here are two examples, but there are endless variations on the same read-my-mind lifestyle theme.

- **Don't ask, don't tell.** In her elementary school years, Mom's father regularly would take her into a men's clothier and sometimes a laundry service business. My mother knew her father did not have anything to pick up at either place, because she was the one who had to wash, iron, and sew his clothes. But he would act as if he had business there and wait until the clerk was not looking and then just walk away with someone else's suit or shirt. My mother asked a few times why he did that, and he just smacked her to the ground. My mother had not read her monster-father's mind to know that he just needed new clothes and was intending to steal them. My maternal grandfather's RTLB was that no one would challenge his ethics or perhaps that he was entitled to steal given his own self-assessment. That rule was forced onto a little girl with no regard for the impact that it would have on her—or me. My mother learned not to steal, but she also internalized the lifestyle that others must read her mind. Those that don't do not understand her needs or value.

- **You love me by knowing what gifts I like and want.** I have a friend whose mother demands they celebrate every birthday and holiday together, even though she rarely engages her daughters personally. The rule-to-live-by here is perhaps, "Families should spend time together to pretend we are all happy and sane on the outside, but I'm going to make sure I get out of them what I want, need, and deserve." My friend's family celebrations are always miserable: sibling squabbles, terrible food, guilt slinging, and other toxic interactions. But, the worst thing is that the mother demands they bring her a gift for her birthday and Christmas. When she opens it, she expresses immediate disappointment that it is not what she wanted. It's not the right brand, not good enough, it doesn't have the right features, it demonstrates that the daughter had not put much thought into the gift, or whatever. Every gift, every time!

This idolatrous lifestyle RTLB bares its ugly teeth on three sisters who walk on glass, are paralyzed with fear of disappointing their mother, and who actually one-up each other for the affections of their mother . . . something that makes that mother beam with control. I still do not completely understand the disconnect between what that mother says ("let's celebrate our family") and what she does (make life miserable for all). Recognizing individual RTLB within a lifestyle cluster sometimes comes from identifying the hypocrisy. It really isn't about the gift, but rather the rules attached to the interactions that function like the strings of a puppet tied around your appendages.

The read-my-mind RTLB have affected me so adversely in two very sad ways. First, I develop even my current relationships around the guilt or angst over whether I'm reading people's minds correctly. I completely second-guess or impugn the motives of the people who love me the most unconditionally. Just like my mother, I do not take what people say or do for me at face value. I do not appreciate it and therefore live constantly in spiritual, emotional, and physical debt to those who offer me Grace, love, friendship, and more in their freest and purest form. And, on the dark flip side, I first overlook when someone truly sins against me and then rage even more than fits the crime when I realize afterwards I've been hurt.

My life now is honestly confronting the negative lifestyle RTLB that create the shame, self-righteousness, and over-obligation I experience as others pursue me.[23] Why would someone do something nice for me? I cannot read their mind, so I impugn their motives. Other RTLB in the same read-my-mind lifestyle cluster keep me from seeing how to reenter the world of loving and serving others with no sense of that same unhealthy, self-centered response. I am a work in progress.

2. Golden Rules

Golden rules are short, pithy sayings that encapsulate a great span of wisdom. The most notable Golden Rule answers the question, "What is the greatest of God's commands in all of the Old Testament Law and Prophets?" Jesus declares that all the Law can be summarized by two commandments—to love the Lord your God with all your heart, soul, mind, and strength, and to love your neighbor as yourself." Since the beginning of Biblical written history, people have lived with this golden rule, but they have decided to live by what THEY believe "loving God" and "loving others" means. They, in essence, have transformed the Golden Rule to mean what they want and not what God meant. Whether you are a person of faith or not, we can all admit that we latch onto these sorts of rules all the time, without even thinking how they control our life and our thinking.

Other rules that function like golden rules have followed a similar pattern. For example, in 409 B.C., Sophocles wrote, "Heaven ne'er helps the men who will not act." From there, in the 17th century, Algernon Sydney, a British politician, penned "God helps those who help themselves." Now, it is a common expression that easily flows off the lips of sacred and secular philosophers alike. These sayings become golden rules by generations of people using them to justify their actions and morals, no matter how toxically people choose to execute those rules.

Over time, individual sayings and beliefs evolve into lifestyle choices. Some families have consolidated their lifestyles RTLB by throwing their favorite golden rules into a melting pot like metallurgy. For example, many people believe "God helps those who help themselves." There's nothing wrong with being self-sufficient and independent to a point. But, this rule is not an excuse for Biblical knowledge (it is nowhere in the Bible). Neither is it a way to deflect our own need to ask for help, nor can we flip the morality and make it an imperative to help others.

It is difficult in any religion or culture to walk past panhandlers without being forced to justify our actions. We can give them money or food or we can walk away. But, in both reactions, we justify our actions by reciting other self-made, personalized golden rules. "Give a man a fish and he'll eat for a day. Teach a man to fish and he'll eat for a lifetime. I'm neither a fisher nor a teacher, so I'm just going to ignore this person." Or, "God helps those who help themselves. There are so many government and nonprofit organizations that this person is not taking advantage of." The consolidated rules are used not only to justify our own actions and judge others, but also to control other people's behavior or dismiss them for being ignorant of the law. This marks the beginning of becoming toxic for and towards others.

Other examples of Golden Rule lifestyle RTLB are:

- **If you've got your health, you've got everything.** This rule emerges when others are complaining about things that make you uncomfortable. "Stop complaining! You are healthy. I don't want to hear anymore. I don't really care about your plight. I have a right to complain more than you since my life is worse than yours." It is a convenient way to dismiss the importance and presence of others.

- **Education is the key to success.** I find this one amusing. In the world's standards, I am quite educated. I have friends who are quite educated. I help marginalized people get educated. And, in my experience, success is not clearly defined. I see people succeed greatly with little or no education. They love their family well. They work hard and honestly. They are patient and kind and not bitter or angry. I also see highly educated people fail miserably due to controllable or uncontrollable circumstances. Some fail because of poor choices and others because they submit to external, toxic RTLB. Others fail because of illness or economic changes. They despair or break apart their families or hit rock bottom for any number of reasons like addiction or greed. These lifestyle rules attempt to puff oneself up or push away the uncomfortable feeling that their personal success may be questionable or immoral or possibly inferior in comparison to other people's.

Still other Golden Rules include:

- Relationships are "give and take." When you do something for others, expect something in return, even if it's that tingly feeling you get for being so paternalistic.

- Don't be indebted to anyone. If they do something nice to you, you must act quickly to return the favor.

- Everything in moderation.

- A man's gotta sow his oats in order to settle down.

- Don't judge me, and I won't judge you.

- Variety is the spice of life.

- If you don't have anything nice to say, say nothing at all.

- Check out any meme on the internet.

- Every generation has it better than the next, and you should be grateful you younger kids have it better than I (one of my mother's most powerful demands for appreciation).

- My mother's pet peeve: Wealthy people can't and don't have good friendships. They are only out for themselves. Any act of generosity from a wealthy person is never enough, because they could be sacrificing more just like me. Never trust a rich person.

When you discover a Golden Rule, or any kind of lifestyle rule for that matter, challenge yourself by asking and answering honest questions. What is the motive behind proclaiming such a rule? How does obeying such a rule help you be a better person? How does enforcing the rule help others? How does the rule help you love others?

3. Social Acceptability

Some lifestyle clusters of rules are so broad or so scripted within our culture and society they are difficult to detect and even harder to challenge. Education can be the key to success, but sometimes that rule can even be a family's arrogant pride and joy, their justification for their own self-righteousness. When these rules are enforced so socially and acceptably, sons may lose their freedom to grow as individuals.

College is not for everyone. Most people know at least one person in one family who was forced into the "education" mold when, clearly, she or he was designed for something else. A stronger and stronger commitment to relying on socially acceptable lifestyle RTLB helps us deny the presence or oppression of the rules themselves. And, it validates our own existence as upright and appropriate but with little or no truth, introspection, empathy, or grace toward others. Examples of socially acceptable lifestyles RTLB that force people into life paths are:

- *"I built this business so you can take over, and you disrespect me for rejecting it."* Or, its converse, *"I built my business so you can have the opportunity to do your OWN thing. This is my thing. If you want to come into this business, you must first jump through the hoops I require, one of which is to go do your business first."* Neither, in and of themselves, forces anyone into a role, but I know third-generation clothiers who just don't want to be in the clothing business. And, I know hard-working young people whose father has made their lives miserable, leaving them no career option or freedom but to work in the family business. Certainly, there is a transparent, less divisive, and more functional way to bring up family members in a business. An overcommitment or unconscious ascent to either of these rules leaves less and less room for healthy relationship and dialogue. In such a toxic environment, we usually resort to our obeying the RTLB and avoid disappointing our parents.

- *As a mother, you must stay at home when your children are young.* Or, its converse, *She's so lazy! Why doesn't she work. She can't make any money staying at home.* Both are misogynist statements. My mother stayed home with us; she did not have her driver's license until I (her youngest) was thirteen years old. Yet, she complained and complained about not having money. She babysat children in her home for a while. Our family hit rock-bottom finan-cially, and she decided to take matters into her own hands. She emasculated my father constantly by reminding him that her first job brought in more than he was making. I also have friends whose children are grown and out of the house. They beam and say "I love being a stay-at-home mom" when the reality is there are no more kids at home and their domestic work is at a minimum as an empty-nester.

And yet, those same moms complain all the time about how tight finances are. Their husbands work hard. One mom I know even received multiple inheritances, but still acts like her husband just doesn't bring home enough, and she hoards money and stuff like the tightest of misers.

Sons must scrutinize socially constructed clusters of RTLB such as this one. The lifestyles are sometimes based on entire philosophies, theologies, social narratives, mythologies, and parenting strategies that guide people away from truthful, meaningful, human connec-tions with each other. What makes a privileged woman with a suc-cessful, loving family moralize and dictate the RTLB, "Your husband should provide for you by giving you a life of freedom from obliga-tions, which includes an abundant luxury of things and experiences to enjoy." Simply because one mom has stayed at home while her husband generated great wealth doesn't mean she is the standard for all women and families. I believe this sort of commitment to stay at home begins to look like idolatry. "Worship me at the foot of the 'Stay-at-home mom' pedestal! Honor me as the role model wife who is 'submissive' to her husband! Watch me exercise all my beau-tiful wisdom from following these oversimplified rules-to-live-by so perfectly." Her perspective is narrow to say the least, and the toxic nature of imposing such a lifestyle RTLB is sad.

- *Spend your youth making connections with the right people (wealthy), and your life will be rosy.* I have a friend who went to a prestigious boarding school to get into a prestigious university to get into a prestigious fraternity to marry the right woman from the right sorority and then get the job with the best of fraternity connections. I've seen him and his wife force the same lifestyle rules onto their children . . . to go to a boarding school, attend a well-connected, expensive camp every summer, get into the best sorority/fraternity at the best institution of higher learning, until the climb brings them to a Nirvana that sets them apart from the riff-raff.

Again, we cannot deny the importance of connections in finding career success. My friend, however, is greatly in debt, living way outside his means, struggles with a drinking problem, and still pledges his allegiance to the make-the-right-connections lifestyle RTLB. After many professional failures and strained friendships, he still concludes he must simply follow these socially acceptable RTLB better or harder or more consistently. In the process, his friends have become his next attempt to stay afloat financially. He is a dear friend to me, and I love and appreciate him. But I grieve when I see his zeal wane hoping that next connection will bring life. Certainly there ought to be a different set of RTLB to help guide us out of this rabbit hole and not further into it.

My mother happened to enforce the converse to this lifestyle rule-to-live-by: *Do NOT spend your life with such-and-so types of people or you'll end up a loser like them.*

- The Jones family are hicks. Their children will never amount to anything. Stay away from them.

- Your friend, Barry, is rich and his parents give him whatever he wants. We don't live like that.

- All the Smith family care about is getting drunk and having more kids. They gotta start taking care of the kids they have and stop making us pay for their welfare. That is NOT how we live!

- All Jane does is flirt, and she lets her daughters do it with any guy that comes off the street. Stay away from people like that!

Mom's adherence to rules like these only confused me as I tried harder and harder to comply with all the other conflicting rules such as, "You have to love everyone for who they are, not for what they have or do." While boundaries are necessary in helping children establish social and individual identities, the Arcuri children didn't know when to discriminate what with whom and for what great moral victory. (What moralistic rule-to-live-by should we be applying now?)

These rules laid the groundwork for my mother to censor my brother's and my friendships quietly and manipulatively. Even more confusing, after an abortion, a drug addiction, a mental breakdown, and a car accident resulting in severe brain injury, my parents let my sister bring home a young man she met at a rock concert. He moved in to my parents' house with my sister, they slept together, and she got pregnant, all the while my mother preaching to my brother that he was living in sin with his then girlfriend. All I learned is to judge others. And even now, I struggle to appreciate a friendship or business relationship without being suspicious or confused.

Overtly praising and reinforcing our RTLB across generations begin to transform and look like less caustic versions of toxicity such as "overbearing or insecure matriarch," "absent patriarch," or "family values." I know of people who hang banners that seem broad and socially acceptable, but it is simply an easy way to mask their myopic view of the world. They pride themselves for living "the better life." But their adherence to vague lifestyle RTLB lets them bask in their self-righteousness and live in their bubble of being educated or being smart or being green or living healthy or living out their political views or being religious or . . . or . . . or . . . .

Socially acceptable RTLB work for most rule-makers and rule-followers most of the time. A family I know is obsessed with people who are smart. The parents do not let their children hang around anyone who is NOT smart . . . according to the parental definition of smart. They subtly keep their children in line so the latter parrot exactly what the former believe: intelligence will be your savior, you are free to judge others' intelligence, you are better than others because of your intelligence (which may or may not be true, but the arrogance is palpable), your need to be intelligent requires you to study in a certain way at a certain institution with censored choices of peers, college major, boyfriends and girlfriends, ethics, behavior, and much more. The children don't even notice the crushing oppressive nature of clustering such intense RTLB into a monolithic lifestyle system.

Yet, both parents and children bask in it! The family projects its rules onto many people with whom they intersect, and they leave those people feeling inferior, judged, and desperate. Outwardly, it is a most noble, socially acceptable pursuit . . . academic and intellectual superiority. But, then they feel free to denounce anything and anyone they deem fundamentalist or who think differently than they. They justify their choice to escape fundamentalist religion, blatantly profiling fundamentalists as unthinking, unintelligent, inferior, or even worse. They have "escaped" from one toxic set of RTLB and replaced them with a superior set—subtler, but just as toxic.

And, outwardly, it works! Obeying a family set of rules-to-live-by can shine brightly on the outside with little effort. The family members' composite life philosophy is outwardly attractive (get educated). But, inside, the toxicity presses on individual psyches, constantly reminding them that their lives are not their own, they cannot perfectly uphold this law or measure up to its standards. Why are we surprised by people who have been secretly numbing their pain with opioids? How is it that most of us can live our lives hiding our intense anger, bitterness, and jealousy of those more fortunate than we? (I once knew a woman who was angry with God—refusing to go to church, or pray or attend church gatherings—because God did not give her twins, but instead just one child!) How can we humans hold a grudge for as long as we live internally justifying our rage and feelings of revenge? My brother did. His anger toward our mother was the last thing he expressed to me before he died thirty-one days after she did.

My personal favorite social acceptability RTLB? "You will like me, affirm me, and validate me as I show you how nice I am. You will do it the way I believe it will bring me life. If you don't, I will despair inwardly and sabotage our friendship with my passive aggression." And, the personal life-giving RTLB I've practiced since I can remember? "I must please my parents or anyone I believe is important. Those people must like me, and I must make myself as useful as possible or they won't appreciate me. If they do not come through for me, then I will ghost them."

Making It Real: A Hodgepodge of Toxic Lifestyle Rules-to-Live-by

When I was four years old, I did something very mean to a cat. My brother ran to save it. He was holding it, comforting it like a seasoned veterinarian. My mother came running and screaming when she heard the cat screeching, and she startled it. The cat writhed, scratched my brother, who released it to run away. My mother picked up a large branch and began to beat my brother. I ran to her crying, pulled on her shorts and said, "Mom, I did that! Mark didn't do that!" She stopped, looked maniacally at me, then at Mark, and proceeded to beat HIM again. She was crying and screaming with rage, "Mark, you should have been watching your brother. You should never have let him do that to that cat." Between beats, she would repeat rule after rule that fell into one or more of the above categories. Read my mind! No matter how young you are, older brothers MUST take care of their younger ones. Honest confession and proper punishment are not as important as unspoken family rules. I should have been watching my kids better. And so on . . . Toxic mothers!

We either create or obey RTLB, ours or someone else's. My brother and I are perfect examples. He and I were completely robbed of adult input during our most formative years. My parents' mantra during that time was, "Your sister is sucking everything out of us, and you two are OK on your own." Mark became driven to prove himself in the business world; I retreated into academia. From 1977 to 1981, we raised ourselves. Mark took an overly responsible role to protect and provide for me, and I, like any fourteen-year-old narcissist, sold weed, enjoyed my life, and completely ignored any sacrifices Mark may have made for me. After high school, we both acquired relative success, but our raw responses to the neglect were very different. Mark stewed on his anger and bitterness and found meaning in himself and his prowess in sales. I plunged into academics and looked for meaning that way. Mark couldn't forgive and it drove him harder and harder to work and to drink. I chose a spiritual journey and counseling to find out why I couldn't escape the judgmentalism, the shame, the rage, the longing for approval, the palpable craving for support.

Neither Mark's nor my approach really helped without proper intervention. Neither of us in our youth had a foundation to guide us in creating healthy, wholesome RTLB. As Figure 1 in Chapter 4 explains, we both escaped our mother's toxic world impulsively, we rejected any moral conscience we had and replaced it with our own morality and we insulated ourselves with people who did not challenge our newly formed but altogether toxic RTLB, and we isolated ourselves so that we were in control of whose rules we would choose to obey. "No one (meaning Mom or Dad or anyone) is ever going to recognize that we two brothers are alive. No one or nothing will fill the void we are constantly trying to fill with meaningless activity and ideas that only we can generate. No one can make up for the fact that our sister's issues stole our parents from us and that now we must simply live without guidance or input. No one is trustworthy. No one is safe. We are to be vulnerable to no one, because that just ends in abandonment and opportunistic people draining us of the only resources we have created."

For me, academic prowess does not go far when you continually blockade your own life with paralyzing shame, self-doubt, and inappropriate anger toward the very ones you claim to love most. For Mark, sales prowess did not go far, either, when the pain of being neglected so intensely for so long only went away with alcohol and rage. Mark and I handled it differently, but the Arcuri lifestyle RTLB kept us both from healing our mother wound.

Perhaps you don't believe this to be true. Perhaps you have already dismissed all this as psycho-babble. Consider, however, that you might be oblivious to your own self-protection and self-justification. You might deny how your shortcomings and your choices are evidence that you are implementing your own RTLB, longing for life like everyone else and trying to define that life the best way you believe possible. Whether you believe it or not, your rules and the way you enforce them affect your family and they force family members to design their own personal RTLB. It truly is a cycle. This is why it is so important to understand that you, yourself, are responsible for your own RTLB, for how they affect others, for changing them if they are toxic, for keeping yourself healthy and continually growing in character and compassion. Hopefully this chapter has helped you begin the journey of identifying your own negative rules and those of your toxic mother. The next chapter will help you choose and create your own more virtuous RTLB.

CHAPTER 7

GENERATING VIRTUOUS LIFESTYLE RULES-TO-LIVE-BY

Breaking Free of Caustic Habits

In order to consider what virtuous lifestyle RTLB look like, sometimes it helps to back into it by examining the toxic ones. As my mother toxically demanded we respect her in the most dysfunctional manner, I developed many clusters of toxic RTLB that haunt me still. I'm still a work in progress, and you'll discover later in this book what to do when you feel the wound is still open or the venom has done irreparable damage. I converted both my mother's sweet encouragement of me when I was helpful and her tyrannical enslavement of punishment when I slacked off in helping with the chores into the best way to avoid her crazy outbursts of anger and abuse. Naturally, when I left, I continued to believe the same RTLB that if I am helpful to someone somewhere, they will like me and appreciate me. My help will make their life easier and I will avoid the awkwardness of finding myself shamed for my inadequacy. In short, I believed it was *life-giving* friendship when I helped others and they stroked my ego as a result. The rule was simple: Affirm me when I am helpful. Acknowledge the sacrifice I've made to help you.

I had designed a whole set of RTLB to convince myself that this is how one made friends and avoided pain. The demand for others to patronize me actually worked against the very life I thought it would bring. No one likes a martyr when there is no need for one. When you help some people, it leaves the door open for them to demand you help more, and my RTLB dictated that I *continue* helping, many times losing myself and any meaningful life-giving moment along the way.

So, a pattern formed; an instinctual habit as natural as breathing. I was helpful, I felt unappreciated, I tried to help again. I felt empty, but I only knew to seek the same life in the same way by following the same rules my mother imposed on me. When that didn't work, my fangs filled with toxic venom as I began judging others unfairly, hurling more and more unspoken rules at them . . . rules that I believed would give me that life I thought I deserved: recognition, accolades, friendship, and all the joy and happiness I assumed everyone else had, but was never part of my story.[24] This pattern is the classic Biblical contrast between Mary and Martha. Mary is blessed to be at the Lord's feet listening, but Martha is angry and bitter that Mary isn't helping her scurry for Jesus' approval. I am a Martha!

A Personal, Modern-Day Illustration

Before such intensive reflection on this dysfunctional pattern I had internalized, I attended a book talk of an author I absolutely love, hosted by a friend who knew of my intense passion for the author and topic too. The friend is quite unorganized and was not at all ready for her guests. In my zeal, I arrived a few minutes early not surprised she was completely unprepared. From my perspective, she passive-aggressively hinted she needed some "desperate help," so I pitched in, conflicted that by helping, I might miss my opportunity to speak informally to the author personally. I set up for the party and guests arrived. She felt comfortable asking me to do more and more, and the author arrived. I continued to fume inwardly that she had better follow my rules to appreciate my sacrifice of service. My jealousy exploded in my heart seeing all her guests except me getting to socialize with the author.

The party happened, the author spoke, the guests chatted, and I chose to help clean up, never having spoken a word to the author. Although my friend did thank me, I was furious, judging her for being selfish for not letting me off the hook for the martyr service I, myself, chose early on to offer. I helped her, and it was supposed to bring me life. I had forgotten she asked me to do it and I said yes. Instead, I sulked and lamented the fact that I couldn't just pursue my own passion like everyone else. Was it my friend's fault that I missed speaking to the author? No! And, by insisting that my RTLB were superior and justifying my toxic reaction to the whole scenario, I robbed myself of ANY joy—friendship with her—and the delight in so many people enjoying the author's message. My overgeneralized rule simply stated, "Sacrifice and you will have life," leaving me incapable of creating any other solutions to loving my friends and pursuing my passions.

Lose the Old. Design the New.

Only when we isolate the RTLB can we see that we place undue burdens on ourselves and others, burdens that result in hurt, pain, stress, and toxicity. When we discover that we've reacted so negatively to the demands of our toxic mothers, we need an approach to design newer, more virtuous RTLB. Remember, the end game is our healing, so some of your more wholesome rules will position you to take care of yourself. But, as Figure 2 suggests, as sons develop an initial set of healthy, virtuous RTLB, we must practice those rules with purpose and intent: finding ways to experience freedom, welcoming healthy input from others, and choosing to live a life of integrity, loving others boldly. So, what do Virtuous Lifestyle RTLB look like? How do we formulate them? We can become more virtuous by design. There are many virtues from which to choose. You get to decide the person you want to become. Remember, your needs, situation, and values will drive which rules you wish to implement how. Any list of virtues seems to overlap with others, and the common virtues fit into packages or families.[25] Sons especially must realize that practicing a virtue almost always requires the consideration of another person's interests. We are not an island. We can choose to behave one way, but we are responsible for how we affect others. Let's examine some of the virtues related to the above scenario. Just how might I have handled that scenario differently?

Virtues Lead to RTLB

Do a google search for "virtues" and you will find lists and descriptions of any virtue you can imagine and more. You'll also find pics and graphic images of lists of hundreds of virtues. What makes us human is that we practice some virtues in some contexts and others in others. For example, Aly McCarthy (2018), in her post for Families of Character,[26] lists 40 virtues and describes them in ranking order in the context of raising a healthy family. The virtue of "habits" tops the list. She also lists "assertiveness" toward the top. She reminds us that "[g]rowing in virtue means forming a new habit and continuing that habit over time."

With honest and personal reflection, I know I do not self-advocate regularly or well, a virtue I am attempting to develop. My toxic mother convinced me early on that I can't assert myself if it takes her away from the spotlight. I need to throw out the belief that stating what I want or need is bad, and people will not like me if I express myself or say no. I would like to create a rule-to-live-by where I engage others in their passions and interests but I do NOT hide my own interests expecting others to read my mind. My friend would have gladly let someone else help her, and we are grown up enough to speak to each other if she feels abandoned. But, I must practice this habit in baby steps in safe environments at first. Life comes when my relationships are strengthened by discussing my needs assertively yet lovingly.

Acts of love, kindness, helpfulness, generosity, and **service,** at least for my personality, all seem to blend together into a cluster of virtues I hope to embody. But my friend neither felt loved or helped after I "blessed her" with my toxic, bitter attitude and assistance. I truly like to help, and I love to be generous. But, when I'm caught off guard, such as when I arrive to the unorganized request for my help or I become surprised by my desire to pursue one of my own interests, I must find a way to be that kind, helpful, loving servant *anyway*, consistently over time.

As a result of neglecting to develop virtues in my youth, my character and integrity gradually devolved into toxic and apathetic, narcissistic pursuits. Upon reflecting on my RTLB, I have discovered that I am usually not aware how much I wish to do something until I have sabotaged my own potential to do it. My mother had conditioned me never to assert my plans. She punished me for her having to work hard and tolerate the hardships at home. I must learn to have the foresight needed to affirm others and enjoy my time with them too. For example, there was nothing but doubt my friend would have been ready for the author. Since I knew she was so disorganized, I should have had the foresight to ask much earlier in the day how I could help. During that time, I could have encouraged her also but let her know how much I was anticipating the gathering and my desire to get the author's autograph. The new, more virtuous RTLB? Life for me and those I interact with comes when I'm able to enjoy my own life by anticipating how I will love and serve those I'm about to see. Notice all the virtues affected by this one scenario.

There was no justice in assuming my friend was intentionally robbing me of my opportunity to meet the author. I didn't have the wisdom, forgiveness and Grace to understand she was simply trying to throw a great party and needed some help. I lost my patience and self-control only when I realized how much I actually wanted to interact with the author and blamed my friend for keeping me from him. I had stuffed what I wanted and how I felt about it, but it was time for me to execute *new* rules, beginning with focusing on how to develop the very virtues I wish to emulate, the ones like those mentioned above that I suppressed because of my own toxic perspective of how life ought to go and be. I can enjoy more meaningful and satisfying relationships (life) if I am aware of my own feelings about situations I am about to enter. When people express what they want and need, it does not mean they are selfish and deserve to be shamed. Neither am I obligated to say yes every time someone asks me for help. Those were my mother's rules. Do the following reflection exercise to begin sensitizing yourself to how you can design your own RTLB that help you to heal and develop personal virtues at the same time.

Think about what it would look like if individual virtues helped guide you to make wise, meaningful decisions for you to become the best version of yourself. In the example, you might see how self-control can allow you to walk away from your toxic mother's abuse before you do something inappropriate or shameful, against the character by which you wish to be known. Why is it important for you to develop more or better self-control? Think about what you would like to gain by having self-control. My new RTLB: "When I am about to interact with my toxic mother, I will first think about my purpose for the interaction and stick to it. Then, I will imagine the consequences of walking away and maintain my dignity and self-control, reminding myself how my mother's toxicity will not change if I stay or if I leave. I am free to do either."

Possible Virtues to Develop[27]

Habits	Acts of Love	Humor	A Better Version of Ourselves
Joy	Orderliness	Generosity	Assertiveness
Courage	Self-control	Helpfulness	Peacefulness
Wisdom	Justice	Modesty	Purposefulness
Forgiveness	Service	Kindness	Responsibility
Good Counsel	Honesty	Respect	Perserverance
Tolerance	Gratitude	Humility	Good judgement
Obedience	Patience	Moderation	Leadership/Command
Truthfulness	Loyalty	Courtesy	Friendliness
Sincerity	Prayerfulness	Greatness	Industriousness
Docility	Foresight	Patriotism	Meekness
Tact	Prudence	Fortitude	Faith
Hope	Discipline	Creativity	Trust
Integrity			

Reflection Exercise: Creating Healthy Rules-To-Live-By

A very important note first! This exercise also works for you to reflect on your own toxic RTLB. Remember, you too have internalized toxic rules and turned them into personal, designer RTLB to impose onto others and for you to indulge the life you believe you deserve. This exercise will assume you can and have done the same reflections for yourself, and details will follow in the next chapters regarding the nature of healing and action points to practice.

What triggers you specifically when you engage your toxic

mother? It won't help if you say something general like, "She's annoying." Think of it more in terms of a rule. Fill in the blank of statements like, "My mother expects me to _____." Or, "My mother assumes that I _____." Or, "My mother lies to me even though we both know the truth, and she explodes toxically on me if I challenge her." Or, "My mother expects me to agree with her even when it goes against everything I stand for."

So, in Column 1, write that trigger in the form of a rule such as in the description above. Remember, we are talking about rules-to-LIVE-by. Next, in Column 2, answer the question, "What life-giving element does she expect to get out of imposing this rule on you?" For example, "When she assumes that I'm motivated by fear of being independent, and when she voices that, she believes I will cower and do what she says, which is usually to stay stuck in the same place I'm already in."

In Column 3, answer HONESTLY, how do you believe this rule is affecting your life? What do you believe will make your life better if you continue to obey this rule? For example, "My mom's toxic RTLB force me to overthink things I want to do in my life, like start a new business or buy a house or get married. I keep believing that she will wake up and realize that she's holding me back from doing the adult things I can and should be doing."

We will assume that you have not experienced life-enhancing, relationship-building experiences from obeying your toxic mother's rule. So, in Column 4, reflect on the list of virtues that follow and write down a few that you feel are compromised because of your engagement with this rule. Another way to think about it is, for example, "If I want to be trustworthy, what is making it difficult in this situation to reinforce the habit (virtue) of being trustworthy?" Or, "I am not practicing **courage** when I choose not to do the grown-up things my mother criticizes." Or, "I am robbed of opportunities to be generous or do loving acts when I try so much to please my mother." Or, "I lack **purposefulness** because I've not had the **discipline** to think it out and make it clear. That's why my mother always knocks me off guard when she belittles my plans."

Now, in Column 5, with the virtue(s) in mind, formulate a rule that brings you health or promotes your better version of yourself.

Make it in the form of a RTLB or a belief that will move you to respond to the situation with more intention and healthy focus. Your new, lifestyle virtuous RTLB might include something like, "I will design a purpose/life statement and review it every time I go into a situation where my mother might humiliate me and my ambitions. I will share it with a friend or mentor and with **discipline**, **sincerity**, and **humility**, will revisit it regularly. When my mother is critical in ways that go against my purpose/life statement, I will excuse myself from the conversation with no shame or guilt."

Notice that when you recreate your RTLB around virtues, the rules end up serving one of many purposes. They can help you heal in specific areas and elevate your personal life. They can also help you heal your relationship with others, even your toxic mother if you so choose. When you know your ultimate goal is to become the best version of yourself with or without your mother, you might even find ways to love your mother in restorative and bold ways (discussed in detail in the next chapter). With lots of work, I put myself on a path of personal healing, but it was not until the last ten years of her life that I chose to move toward her with bold love. Remember, as shown in Figure 2 from Chapter 4, you have the rest of your life to create and refine these virtuous lifestyle RTLB while celebrating a newfound joy and freedom the new rules generate. In addition, that freedom can launch you to form new habits, hobbies, and relationships with others. And ultimately, you will grow in your ability to develop an integrity of which you can be proud and an ability to love anyone you choose boldly, restoring them to a better relationship with themselves, with others, with you, and with God.

Worksheet:
Creating Healthy Rules-To-Live-By

Mom's Rule, My Trigger	She Expects What?	The Rules' Impact on Me	Virtues Affected	Healthy, Virtuous Rules-to-Live-by
EXAMPLE: I have suffered more than you because I came from a poor background. I gave you a great life so any suffering you have or suggestion that I have contributed to that suffering is selfish and meaningless. You disappoint me when you don't affirm my wisdom and advice.	My mother wants to be absolved of the guilt and shame both of her own childhood and the abuse and neglect in parenting me that she denies.	When she forces me to agree and I give in, then her fantasy is reinforced, she feels empowered and delivered from the guilt of her toxicity and then is armed for the next time at an escalated level.	Assertiveness, courage, honesty, gratitude, forgiveness, trust, and respect (for her and myself)	I am free to disagree with her regarding her toxic treatment of me. To heal and develop, I will arm myself with a few memories for which I am thankful. I must have the courage and trust that my life is in my control even if she withdraws resources and attention from me, even if she actively tries to humiliate me. I do not have to apologize for having a different perspective of how my toxic mother treated and treats me. Forgiving her and respecting her does not mean I cannot forgive myself and respect the man I am and the progress I am making. By being assertive when I walk away, I will trust that God will take care of me. I will build a group of supportive friends whom I can respect and who respect me.

Later in this book, we will examine how we can judge the quality and sustainability of the new, healthy, virtuous rules-to-live-by in a special way that help sons build integrity. Our RTLB are contributing to our growth and healing when those rules facilitate our loving others boldly.

CHAPTER 8

ARMED WITH VIRTUE, ENTER YOUR WORLD EQUIPPED

If you have worked hard at creating healthy and virtuous RTLB, then you are equipped to step freely and safely into the world and begin healing. The process depicted in Figure 2 encourages us to walk intentionally into three different areas of our own personal spaces. Whether it is with your mother or with your self-selected, isolating, and insulating peers, you have been imprisoned in a floating cage made of very thin glass. You have been afraid to move too far within the cage for fear that the walls would crack or shatter. At one point in every son's life, our cage is shattered, whether from terminal illness, death, divorce, our personal failures, our mother's own cruelty, or any number of other tragedies.

Before designing your own virtuous lifestyle RTLB, you were burdened as much by your attempts to escape your toxic mother's influences as you were trying to resist becoming toxic yourself. There are three guiding, equipping principles to keep in mind as you practice even the smallest rule-to-live-by. At least one of these principles must frame your healing step, whether it is a baby step or a giant leap. Let's consider each principle separately, but your maximum healing will be to integrate them into your everyday life, thoughts, habits, and plans.

Principle 1: Enjoy Your Freedom

Let your newly acquired freedom include creativity in dreaming big and little joys for you and those you wish to love.[28] Let it inform your decisions to pursue your interests and the interests of others. The more you experience joy in ways that bring you confidence, the better equipped you are to handle your toxic mother and all the buttons she pushes.

Heed These Warnings!

There's a big difference between joy and vice-seeking, and the line is blurred unless we have perspective. Beware of three things! First, think long and hard about what you wish to enjoy. Drugs? Probably not! Isolating or insulating yourself with that former small set of friends you recruited whom you now know do *not* encourage you in the newfound ways you wish to grow? No, thank you. But, how do you "enjoy" their company?

I have a friend who created an "8-pack." It was so named because it consisted of four couples who drank to oblivion every time they got together, even encouraging their children to drink and smoke at an early age. Insulated in a suffocating bubble? Of course? No one challenged the status quo. Did it bring joy and create the kind of person my friend wanted to be? I'm not the judge, but you can be.

When one man in the 8-pack decided he had a drinking problem and needed to begin a 12-step program, guess what the rest of the 8-pack did, including my friend and his wife? Did they rally around their friend with an addiction problem? Did they sacrifice a bit to bring this struggling friend some joy *without* alcohol? NO! They kicked the husband and his wife out of the 8-pack and became a 6-pack. They didn't want to feel judged by his need to abstain from alcohol.

This is NOT the kind of joy we should pursue, unless that is the kind of "friend" we wish to be. But, if we have first mapped out what kind of friend we want to become, then our choices to react to things while we pursue virtue and joy help reinforce and build us into a better man, and hence, a better son, husband, and father. Regarding this scenario, I want to be a person whose joy AND freedom come from bringing others joy, healing, and freedom.

Second, walking into a dangerous situation with a haphazard, naïve or hedonistic sense of joy opens the door for the toxic mother to enter with a vengeance. You may decide not to allow your mother to sabotage your love of music and learning. So, you choose to pursue the joy and pride of mastering the guitar. If you simply approach your toxic mother with a "Mom, I'm not gonna take your crap anymore. Instead, I'm gonna to learn to play the guitar," she will eat you for lunch. This means you must learn the art of boundaries.

Boundaries are intended to protect and, hopefully change *you* for the better. They are never intended to punish or change the toxic offender. If you are unfamiliar with what boundaries are or how to form them, then please seek guidance from a professional. It is up to you to equip yourself with healthy boundaries. A toxic mother knows when to step over your boundaries to maintain the control she believes she needs. And, if she doesn't know she is doing it, then you probably need even stronger boundaries. A small illustration might help.

Here is an anecdotal illustration.

Bring Joy Where You Can

My father suffered a great deal at the hand of my toxic mother, but they chose to stay together. She preyed on his vulnerabilities of health and infidelity to make his life a misery. My father loved to collect coins, but he really didn't have the finances to do it to the level he wished. When I discovered this, I offered to take him to a couple of coin shows with my secret plan of letting him pick out a few of his missing coins to complete his sets.

My mother despised that I interacted with my father with joy and excitement since it appeared to thwart her plan to imprison my father. I had created a boundary and RTLB that helped me move freely into a world where my father and I were once trapped. I wanted to be generous and gracious, happy for someone else's successes, instrumental in bringing others joy. These were the virtues I wanted to cultivate in myself, and I was going to practice them by loving my father.

In reaction to me pursuing a common interest with my father, my mother regularly brought up the fact that my solution to everything was money, that I was materialistic, and that I shouldn't interfere with my father's collecting. But, I had, to her dismay, decided I was going to experience joy with at least one of my parents while they were living. AND . . . I was not going to let my mother rob me of it. (That was my boundary.)

So, I called him regularly to find out the status of his sets. I plotted and schemed for the next time I would see them . . . during my son's ninth grade play, in which he was the lead. I bought my father a few Morgan Dollars he was missing and presented them to him. My father laughed with joy. My mother? "Guy, you know we can't afford stuff like this! You can't keep buying us stuff just because you think we want it." I looked at her (almost in spite) and handed my father ANOTHER coin, and another! I said, "Mom, Dad loves spending time piddling with his coins, and I love that. If he wants, he can give them back or he can sell them, probably for more than I bought them." My dad walked out of the room and immediately stuffed the coins into his suitcase, making sure they would not be scratched or dented. Obviously, I had hit a home run in the coin/joy department. He was all smiles.

Growing in Virtue

We ended up filling in almost every one of his holes for his coin series and sets for another four years until he died. When he was in palliative care, I was staying at home with my mother while she decided whether to remove him from life-support. When we returned home from the hospital after he died, the first thing my mother did was hand-deliver my father's coin collection to me and tell me she wanted me to have it. And, NOT out of spite but because I had kept working on my virtue in this context, the next thing I did was to appraise it and hand her a check for the amount.

I believe she had learned a small lesson on the benefits of joy by offering it to me, and I wanted her to be the beneficiary of her husband's assets as she was entitled. But my boundary was put in place to heal me as much as to help me become virtuous. I vowed early on in my mother's toxic approach to my dad's joy and his hobby never to let her give me something with strings attached. In that moment, I believed it better for her to benefit financially from that collection first and foremost.

I had become free enough from my toxic mother to create joy both for myself and my father. And, I was free enough not to interpret the joy of inheriting the collection as a "payment" for her toxicity toward my father and me. It was a sweet adventure of practicing my own virtue of being generous and encouraging in the midst of my newfound freedom.

There are unlimited opportunities to test the health of your freedom and boundaries, most of which do not involve your toxic mother. Resurrect an old hobby or begin a new one. Meet people with the same interests through those hobbies or other social groups such as church, sports leagues, travel, schooling, or professional development. Arm yourself with your RTLB and break free of the chains. As you interact with others, you can tweak and revise your RTLB.

And the third warning. As you practice entering the world with a virtuous and healing purpose, remember you are human. You make mistakes. Your stepping out freely from the imprisonment you were experiencing will inevitably fall flat and perhaps hurt others or even yourself. Do not give up. Whatever your faith, you must know the power of forgiveness and Grace. Everyone benefits from unconditional love and secular research has touted the benefits of forgiving, forgiveness, and not holding grudges. If you cannot break away from the imprisonment of self-doubt, self-sabotage, self-contempt, self-ANYTHING, then seek professional help. This brings us to the second guiding principle to healing.

Principle 2: Welcome Healthy Input from Others

Your newfound lifestyle of freedom must also embrace a vigilance to gather a healthy support team—a group of cheerleaders who have your best interests at heart. This can include professional counselors, therapists, clergy, authors, trusted friends, confidants.[29] All of these "family members" can be conduits to healthy input to apply to your personal healing. For example, counselors can recommend books by authors who have healthy perspectives on your issues and even discuss them in therapy.

In fact, there are intensive support groups and counseling group services that remove you completely from a toxic situation to provide you with a set of people who will speak truth and love into your life with power but with complete confidentiality. For example, there are retreat groups for intensive marriage counseling or for support in treatment for addiction to anything (pornography, sex, drugs, food, toxic relationships, you name it.).[30] All these people and resources can be part of your support team while you step into the free world to exercise your RTLB. They can equip you with the help you need.

A Shout-out to Ralph Isaacson: My Surrogate Father

Some Background

With healthy scrutiny, you can benefit from a unique support from a mentor or, in my case, a surrogate father. At this point, you may realize how toxic my mother was, even though you do not know her whole nightmare childhood story, one that made her create RTLB that she imposed on her whole family. She was not 100 percent evil, but she wrecked our lives repeatedly. And yet, there is an untold story here. My father was absent the whole time: physically, emotionally, relationally, and mentally. While she beat him down, he withdrew into his own world of infidelity and shame. When he wasn't working, he was carousing. When we struggled personally, he did not engage. As children, he did not defend us from our toxic mother.

Mom would manipulate him to speak to us about morals and ethics even though she didn't agree with his nor the way he chose to discuss them with us. For example, in front of my brother and me, Mom told my father to "give [us] the talk AGAIN because [he] didn't do it right the first time." He took us into my bedroom and said, "Look, you can have sex with whoever you want, but, if you're gonna have sex, wear a condom. You don't want to have children or get a disease before you get married." And then he told us not to tell our mom what we discussed. In short, my father did not model for me the kind of man I began realizing I wanted to be as a married, young adult.

I Needed a Father Too

In counseling for infertility and marriage issues, my therapist counseled my wife and me together, but we soon discovered I needed individual help to work on how I retreat and handle anything from disappointment to pain to friendship to almost everything. She realized early on that I needed a father-figure role model on my team—to demonstrate what it means to be a man of integrity, of health, of love and care for others, and so much more. It so happened that her father did just that for many other men.

Enter my counselor's father, Ralph Isaacson. He heroically had trained himself to be a mentor for prisoners and for anyone who would commit to being honest with him. He lived his life reflecting God's unconditional love as well as he could on this side of heaven. God knows our deepest, darkest pain and shame, and He still loves us. Ralph listened to my life atrocities, and he accepted me just as I was. He was shocked at some of my stories, but his only reaction was, "Guy, I don't need to hear these stories as much as you need to tell them." He understood that I could begin to shed the stigma of such toxicity simply by telling someone the truth out loud.

Sometimes he would laugh at my stories, at how "gross" they were, but in the most encouraging context that I was such a survivor—successful in so many ways. For nine years, we met weekly.

He listened to my wretched past and my pathetic response to it in my present. He challenged the toxic manner in which I responded to my wife, my disdain for my incompetent boss, and more. In essence, he was helping me identify the toxic RTLB I had personally created or internalized from my mother. Ralph helped me see that I had completely rejected my conscience and my former life, living a fantasy that I was creating better circumstances for myself. He showed me how I had taken the easy and subconscious way out, escaping my parents' influences impulsively. He showed me that I had substituted a different life and RTLB to run my life, but the control I felt was simply because I had isolated myself from one toxic environment and insulated myself into a bubble of people who would never know or see the pain and rage in my own heart.

He was the first one to introduce me to personality tests, and that served as the beginning of my ability to examine the darkness of my own heart. BUT, he immediately called me out for sugarcoating my healing. I was framing my newer, healthier patterns with Christian-ease, flowery, religious language, counseling terms and concepts that made me seem "cured." I was simply looking for another quick fix.

He looked right past that. I was arrogant about understanding the roots of my toxic nature, and it all pointed to my mother. He simply said, "Guy, you can have all the wisdom and understanding of why you are so messed up, but that doesn't excuse you from loving God or loving others well. Just because you know the cause of your dysfunction doesn't mean you will create a life for you and your family without dysfunction. You've got to learn how to take responsibility for what you can take responsibility for."

Then, he would offer unconditional love, acceptance and Grace . . . and freedom and safety to explore how to become a better person in the midst of all the dirty laundry we had hung out together to examine. We read books together and discussed their application to my life, helping me redefine who I wanted to be instead of this shameful, sad, and imprisoned man. He shared his own thinking and his own life decisions, his successes and failures, and their impact on his life and family roles now—retired, grown children, grandfather, husband. He became my surrogate father, but he served that role for many, many other men over the years! As you will see later, I wanted to be like him and orchestrated my life and RTLB to grow into a man of integrity like Ralph Isaacson. I now mentor young men in the same capacity.

Principle 3: Develop Integrity and Love Boldly

As we step into a world with new RTLB, we are boldly going where no son has gone before. It looks very similar to the same old life bubble until we begin to exercise our newfound freedom with joy and vision to become a better man. When we encounter difficulty or conflict while attempting to pursue our own interests and heal from the pain and wounds we've sustained from our toxic mothers, we make sure we are welcoming appropriate feedback and input from trusted sources. This is the beginning of becoming a man of integrity. It takes effort and discipline to transform ourselves into people who can love and be loved well. To do this, we must first have a clear sense of what it means to live with integrity. But, second, men must also have a road map—a clear measure of whether they are growing that integrity. That measure is love.

The third and final principle to guide us into a world of healing is that we sons are the only ones responsible for the kind of healing that we want. I believe healing comes from intentional development of integrity with the goal of determining how well we are loving others and being loved. As we refine and define ourselves with virtue, we must stay true to ourselves. This is an issue of integrity, but I've rarely seen boys or even young men being taught how to maintain their own integrity, especially in the context of living well in community.

Developing Integrity

Integrity means a lot of things to a lot of people. If we are going to grow and heal confidently, we must know what it looks like to develop integrity. Human behavior is easier to change when we see concrete examples. Merriam-Webster[31] defines integrity as

1. firm <u>adherence</u> to a code of especially moral or artistic values: <u>INCORRUPTIBILITY</u>

2. an unimpaired condition: <u>SOUNDNESS</u>

3. the quality or state of being complete or undivided: <u>COMPLETENESS</u>

We must embrace our healing with our new "code of moral values," or RTLB. We must know that those rules are "sound" so that we don't fall into the trap of smug self-righteousness or escapism or even a vulnerability to become legalistic or victimized again.

And, we must vigilantly fight to keep ourselves "complete," with our attention to healing "undivided."

So, we need a litmus test to know if our integrity is developing the way we planned. We need a road map to let us know we are progressing toward sustainable healing. With our integrity at stake, we must walk into the world in which we want to find healing with the same incorruptible, sound, and complete commitment to heal others. And that way is Bold Love. Are we being loved boldly? Are we loving others boldly? What does Bold Love look like, anyway?

Bold Love

Early in my marriage I learned through counseling that I can only control myself, I am not responsible for what other people say or how they react toward me. I can now try my best and ask for forgiveness and try to do or be better when I hurt someone. I was, however, accustomed to blaming my toxic mother for my woes, my failures, my limitations and my immaturity. I justified how poorly I treated others. My guiding principles were simply judgment: I was going to do life better than this. I was going to have a beautiful marriage. I was going to be an amazing father. I was going to encourage my children to get an education. I was going to have great friends and respect them.

But, at age twenty, I had not thought through my need for new RTLB, nor did I understand the integrity on which I was basing my horrible approaches to love my wife and my friends. This all became apparent when Marie and I decided to have children. After three miscarriages and a diagnosis that her genetic condition was already sending her through early menopause, my world began to implode. Our marriage was strained. My dreams were challenged. I was bankrupt emotionally to love my wife or others. I was, as James 3:4 says, like a ship without a rudder.

> [4] Or take ships as an example. Although they are so large and are driven by strong winds, they are steered by a very small rudder wherever the pilot wants to go (NIV).

I was stuck—not even having admitted I was toxic toward those I loved. I needed to rebuild my rudder. I needed a new definition of love. One that would free and not enslave. One that would inspire and not demand conformity. My mother taught me the latter, and I needed input to create new RTLB. I discovered that definition . . . that principle . . . in a book by Dan Allender, *Bold Love*. Allender's principle of bold love transcends any relationship and any circumstance. In my words, Allender describes bold love like this: *Bold Love is the conscious act of restoring another person to a better relationship with themselves, with you, with others and/or with God.*

What does this mean?

We must equip ourselves with the ability to love boldly. Our newly forming virtuous, lifestyle RTLB are validated by honestly assessing whether they equip us to love others or ourselves boldly. Nothing more, nothing less! Every rule and every virtue you would like to see become part of your character depend on your attempts to love boldly. As you step into your world, your healing begins when you learn to love boldly and intentionally. Progress may be seen in tiny steps and not necessarily in the contexts you imagine. You may choose to love your toxic mother boldly in some situations and have it completely backfire. Or, you may walk freely equipped into a situation where you intend to love one person boldly and end up loving someone else. You may reach out to help a friend and find he doesn't want that help.

You have been designed to love and be loved, but you can only concentrate on how you love, not how others choose to love you or receive that love. So, it is crucial that you understand you are loved by God and forgiven with Amazing Grace, whether your decision to love someone or your construction of RTLB are the best ways to love anyone or not. God loves you unconditionally, and you have built a support family that demonstrates that love in the best way possible. This frees you to love, forgive, and ask for forgiveness in bold ways.

Even if you are not a person of faith, your object of love should always be approached with intentional restoration in mind. Will your act of love help others to reconcile with themselves? Can you help them improve their relationship with you or another? Is the way they believe they are loving you helping you to understand and accept yourself or others unconditionally? It is up to you to allow your creativity and your RTLB to orchestrate the redemptive, restorative act of bold love.

This Bold Love test now helps you understand the appropriateness of withdrawing when you are being abused and humiliated, when you realize with humility and compassion that you are not loving boldly or are not being loved boldly. Don't forget you also need to love and forgive yourself. You also need to open yourself up to be loved boldly. By stepping out into the world equipped to love and be loved, bold love becomes the litmus test for whether your healing is progressing in the proper directions. When stepping out brings you to that awkward point where you don't feel your RTLB are functioning, ask yourself some questions.

1. Is this awkward because it is so new for me to be doing this?

2. Do my RTLB help me anticipate how I can restore others to a better relationship to themselves, me, others, or God?

3. Am I willing to accept rejection? Am I willing to admit to this other person or myself that I might be approaching this sort of reconciliation (bold love) the wrong way?

4. What are my motives for attempting to love this person boldly? Are those motives tainted by my self-righteousness, arrogance, sense of revenge, or any other negative character trait fighting against the virtues I'd like to see as part of my character?

5. Do I understand the whole situation? Are there other factors or people to consider?

6. Do I need more empathy or sympathy to love or be loved boldly?

7. Am I OK with the potential that the person I choose to love will find restoration with someone else and perhaps still cast their toxic RTLB on me?

Integrity and Bold Love: A Two-Sided Anchor

In exercising your newfound freedom to step into the world and find healing, remember that a life of loving and being loved boldly is your goal. Integrity serves as one side of the anchor to your life, helping you stay grounded in the midst of uncharted territory. If integrity is the consistent practice of the virtues you have decided to be part of your RTLB, then bold love is the other side of that anchor. Bold love digs itself into the soft sand of your newly formed RTLB, providing the appropriate tension on your lifeline as you focus your RTLB on the restoration of others and yourself to better relationships in rough and dangerous seas. It is important that you understand how your perceptions of love affect your ability to stay on the path of healing. To move out into your world equipped, you must make sure your anchor is properly attached.

The Greatest of These

Applying the definitions of integrity and love, I Corinthians 13: 1-7 sets me up not only to heal, but frees me to choose to love anyone I want—from my wife to my friend to my toxic mother. I'm making progress if my RTLB are guiding me to love someone boldly. Read these very familiar "wedding ceremony" verses of love aloud. Every time you see the word "**love**" or "**it**" bolded, replace it with a form of the definition "consciously restore others to a better relationship with themselves, with me, with others, and/or with God." See the example below and then recite for yourself the whole passage with the bold love substitution.

> [1]If I speak in the tongues of men or of angels, but do not have **love**, I am only a resounding gong or a clanging cymbal. [2]If I have the gift of prophecy and can fathom all mysteries and all knowledge, and if I have a faith that can move mountains, but do not have **love**, I am nothing. [3]If I give all I possess to the poor and give over my body to hardship that I may boast, but do not have **love**, I gain nothing.

> [4]**Love** is patient, **love** is kind. **It** does not envy, **it** does not boast, **it** is not proud. [5]**It** does not dishonor others, **it** is not self-seeking, **it** is not easily angered, **it** keeps no record of wrongs. [6]**Love** does not delight in evil but rejoices with the truth. [7]**It** always protects, always trusts, always hopes, always perseveres.[32]

> EXAMPLE: [1]If I speak in the tongues of men or of angels, but I do not **restore others to a better relationship with themselves, me, others, or God**, then I am only a resounding gong or a clanging cymbal . . . . [4]**To restore others to a better relationship with themselves, me, others, or God** is patient . . . kind . . . .

So, what can we learn by doing this exercise? With Allender's definition to frame these verses, you can begin to make moral and behavioral decisions to love, restoring those you wish to love to better, healthier relationships. You can keep yourself and your attitude in check by remembering what love looks like. When attempting to love your toxic mother boldly, for example, these verses become tangible when you plan. Let's examine each paragraph of verses in this manner and see how integrity and bold love can remain at the forefront of our healing process no matter whom we choose to love.

Paragraph 1, Verses 1-3: No matter how eloquently I can tell my toxic mother she is wrong or hurtful, no matter how spiritually true I think I am stating my case to my toxic mother, no matter how much I convince her I am growing spiritually or emotionally, and no matter how much I give to my toxic mother, two things are true.

First, if I do not do them with the motivation to restore her to a better relationship with herself, with me, with others, or with God, I am not loving her, and I ought to abstain. This gives me the freedom **and safety** to try to love as much as the encouragement to stop wasting my efforts where I should.

Second, it is not up to me to restore those relationships; it is God's. He requires me in these verses simply to love, not to make my toxic mother become a nice person to me. My success and results do not depend on my gain of anything such as money, status, peace, mom's affection, etc. Instead, my success is simply that I obeyed and loved. I do not have to change nor do I have to judge my toxic mother.

Verses 4-7: Restoring another person to a better relationship with himself, herself, you, others, or God requires patience and kindness. It requires us not to envy, boast, not to dishonor our mother, get angry with her, nor to hold things against her. This has been the hardest for me as I write this book. I still today detect my anger and bitterness toward my mother. I am a work in progress, thanks be to God! This kind of love requires us to rejoice in truth and not to delight in evil. Remember, we must take the log out of our own eye before we concern ourselves with the speck in another's.

Step one of this healing process is to take ownership of our personal toxicity. As we attempt to restore our toxic mother to a better relationship with herself, others, us, or God, we must remember that God is in control, not us. He will protect us as we protect our integrity and motivation to love boldly. We can hope, trust, and persevere knowing that God has much greater in mind both for us and for our toxic mother.

Real-Life Struggle to Love

Now I know why I am to be patient. I can plant seeds with my children or even in myself to love others and be generous without expecting to get it right every time. Now I know why I am not to envy. Because it is not only putting enmity between me and the one I envy, but it does not help my toxic mother love herself better or love others better.

Speaking of envy, I have always wanted to be a father. As I was learning to love boldly, I stepped out to cultivate that love of children in restorative ways. When all of our friends were having children, I was able to keep my pain of infertility in check while being the best "uncle" a kid could ever have. I babysat with joy so my wife could go out with her friends who had recently given birth. Yes, I even wore the badge of vomit on my shirt as they came back from their outing.

The pain of being childless did not subside, however. I was secretly harboring anger and bitterness at others and even at God that my efforts to love children did not bring me the life I felt I deserved: to be a father. My RTLB were the subtle demand that people respect my wisdom and ability to parent even though I had no children of my own. I recognized early on and through counseling that I was seeking personal validation through other people's affirmation of my work with children.

Helping children succeed was supposed to bring me life-giving energy and happiness. I needed a way to continue practicing the virtue of helping schools, churches, and parents do their best with children without believing my self-worth came from other people's opinions, even though I was an expert in education of children birth to 12th grade. I needed to believe I was loved unconditionally, and my work needed to have bold love as the center focus.

I continued to teach children's Sunday school and started an independent K-8 school with very fertile people. The parents of these children I served were spitting out children like loose teeth every nine months. Yes, I grieved when ignorant mothers would challenge my PhD in Education and ask me why I should know anything about children since I didn't have any of my own. But, I "believed all things." I was patient. I was as kind as I could be in public, but, yes, in my heart I was angry and envious and to this day I remember who those ignorant people are. No one can love like this perfectly except God, and that is why my attempt to love boldly must include my own faith and trust in the God of the Universe. He forgives my imperfect love and even redeems it to restore His own people to a better relationship with themselves and with Him.

Bold Love Takes a Surprising Turn: Assessing Your Ability to Love Boldly

It takes humility and integrity to assess whether you are loving boldly. My mother knew it all. She would tell you that. She would correct you when your world did not agree with hers. She would insist that her perspective, her knowledge, her wisdom superseded anything outside Hazel World. She did not examine her life or the impact she had on others, and she lost the ability to love others boldly and inter-personally. Since my mother lived alone in Hazel World, she did not need to reflect, humble herself, nor take ownership for loving and being loved.

"Matriarch" seems to be an appropriate word here. If you obsessed over Netflix's *The Crown* like I did, you might have become outraged when Elizabeth simply dictated her sister's life and happiness. No matter what the input, the queen simply laid down the rule, and it was so! My mother said she gets input from others, but, her decisions were made in the vacuum of isolation and insulation since the day she ran away from home at fifteen years old. It didn't matter how devastating or irrational the blow, she said it and that settled it!

One late February, Marie and I invited my parents to come to our house in Winston Salem. Mom had told me I never come home, that I was selfish, that I hadn't celebrated my father's birthday (Valentine's Day) in a long time, that I was depriving her of her grandchildren, that I was embarrassed to be around them because they aren't rich or educated, that they couldn't get away because they couldn't be that far away from my sister and her kids (remember the envy principle?), and much more not worth mentioning. We invited them to come, stay with us, attend BOTH productions of our son's play in which he was the lead and to celebrate Dad's birthday.

With the enthusiasm of a snail, they came. All my mother did was complain that my family goes out to eat too often, that we have a cluttered house, that I wouldn't let her clean but she couldn't stand the clutter, that we are too permissive in our parenting, that our children are sooooo much more privileged than their cousins. I think you get the picture. She was discontent and driving the very points I thought I had addressed by offering for them to visit.

One evening, she disappeared and we discovered her rummaging through some pictures in the basement. Marie and I had been deep into making Creative Memories books and had laid out an entire album of my childhood. My mother came up the stairs, stopped at the entrance, and called me. Not just a friendly "Hey, Guy," but an ominous, angry, deep "Guy, come here now!" I did not call out but ran to her, thinking one of our kids had exhibited that dreaded "spoiled brat" behavior my mother constantly pointed out to me and to them, unsolicited. This time, however, she put a flat box of pages for the album in my face like a disgruntled pizza delivery man.

I immediately conjured my RTLB I *thought* would handle this situation. I wanted to love my mother boldly, but the stars did not align! Instead, I ended up pulling out a *different* set of RTLB, able to love my wife boldly by intentionally being passive, not proactive or aggressive. THIS was a victory in healing, for sure!

"Guy, I want these!"

This is all she said. I played stupid.

"Oh, yeah! Marie and I are making albums with all of our pictures."

I detected the detonator, set to explode any moment, but I was hopeful my plan of action would work. I intended to execute my RTLB that helped me deescalate her rage by reflecting a joyful perspective of what she presents to me. Instead of reacting to her negative humiliation and condescending approach to communication, I wanted to reflect that I was choosing to be joyful in the things over which she demanded control.

"I want these pictures. They are mine."

With a smile and an invitation to go back to the basement to see our other scrapbook pages, I replied, "No, Mom. These are the duplicates of the originals you gave us. Remember, we gave you back the originals."

"I want these pictures, and you are going to give them to me. I'm the matriarch of this family and I can have whatever I want."

You may be thinking, "No, she didn't say that! That's way too bizarre. It sounds like a scene in *The Exorcist*." Remember, toxicity is the enforcement of your RTLB in inappropriate ways that demand that others comply and bring you the life you believe you deserve. I hope by now you can see her RTLB had crossed way too many boundaries.

By this time Marie had heard the absolute raging madness in her voice, and I knew this conversation wasn't over. I cringed, but at that moment I knew out of bold love for my wife I needed to cue up a different set of RTLB. I was going to defend whatever came out of Marie's mouth! I thought it was more important to maintain and restore my relationship with Marie than with my mother, who was out of control and toxic. I was ready to walk away from my relationship with my mother over pictures because I could not predict how Marie would react. Marie had every right to react however she wished, and I was going to defend my wife no matter what! My relationship with Marie is much more important than with my mother.

"No, Hazel, these are ours. We've been working on these for a long time."

"Marie, this is none of your business. He's MY son, and I say I want these pictures."

I love my wife and am in awe of her confidence and strength. I assumed she was ready to fight for those pictures, and I would heed the battle call with every artillery I had designed to defend my amazing wife. No matter WHAT she chose to do or say, I was on her side. The red glaze in my mother's eyes, however, were Satan's headlights, and Marie conceded and walked away.

Here's the saddest part. My father witnessed all this and did nothing while Mom fumed and robbed us of our pictures. As Mom went upstairs to put the box of pictures in her suitcase, my father spoke up. His private and whispered conversation was as weak as his refusal to step into the craziness of a classic Hazel World interaction.

"Guy, she's mad at me because I'm just sitting around wanting to watch TV."

We didn't have a great TV then, and it was hard to watch, and Marie and I didn't want to do the same thing we do when we visited them four states away: watch TV 24/7! Was that his excuse or a statement that we should have a better TV for him when he visits?

The bottom line? Marie humbled herself and gave up several weeks' worth of work. I humbled myself only by knowing in THAT moment, I was prepared to respect and defend my WIFE, even if it meant driving a wedge between my toxic mother and me.

I didn't restore my mother to a better relationship to anyone, but, in trying to do so, I was able to love my wife, communicating to her my gratitude for her sanity and her backing down, and she was grateful knowing I would protect her from my mother's lunacy EVERY time and defend Marie's decision to be herself in the midst of Mom's venom. I am not responsible for my mother's sputum nor my father's passivity, but in trying to practice bold love with my mother, I simply clung to my wife, restoring us both to trust more in each other and in God. Enough said!

EXERCISE: Fill in the four blanks around each of the three principles or contexts with which to implement your virtuous rules-to-live-by. Brainstorm possibilities to enjoy your freedom. Consider carefully the sources that you trust to help you grow in virtue and heal well. Write down the names of people you believe love you boldly or whom you wish to do the same. Do you feel better equipped to move out into your world?

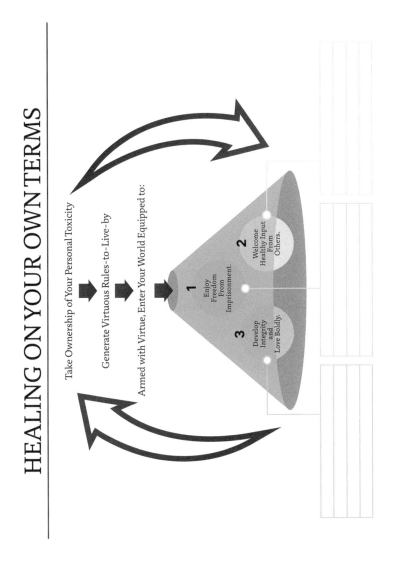

HEALING ON YOUR OWN TERMS

Take Ownership of Your Personal Toxicity

Generate Virtuous Rules-to-Live-by

Armed with Virtue, Enter Your World Equipped to:

1 — Enjoy Freedom From Imprisonment.

2 — Welcome Healthy Input From Others.

3 — Develop Integrity and Love Boldly.

SECTION 3

Healing Tips

CHAPTER 9

HEALING WHAT MATTERS

I had a difficult time choosing a title for this book. "Moving on" seemed a bit harsh, but "surviving" stripped sons of the possibility of joy in relationships. Toxic mothers move on whether they continue their collateral damage on their sons or not. But they rarely heal from their own wounds or change into healthy, loving humans without personal commitment and responsibility. Sons can heal in spite of our toxic mothers, and we can move on. We can move on with or without our toxic mothers because we are striving to build virtuous character in spite of our mother's refusal to examine her life. Even though we did not experience the maturity of an emotionally healthy mother, we do not have to dwell on the hurt and pain. We can move on.

A destructive *mother* sometimes despairs when her son moves on, but a mature mother celebrates her son's independence and self-reliance.[33] It is bittersweet, for sure, but his autonomy frees the mature mother to move on herself while choosing how to support her son when he welcomes or asks her. An immature *son* moves on in the way we showed in Figure 1. He succumbs to the control and manipulation of his toxic mother or he rejects it with little or no help in stopping the madness or its effects on him. A mature son moves on with hope in his heart and a plan in his head whether his mom is toxic or not. By maintaining his integrity and loving boldly, a mature son can and will find effective ways to heal. What matters for a son is to heal what matters!

Here are some contexts that might help you work on your

healing. They represent a compilation of everything in this book and a whole lot more research on how sons can heal themselves from their mother wounds. These categories are not exhaustive. They are ways to provide you some context and focus for where you might begin your healing. Hopefully this list will encourage you to work consistently. Many of the contexts overlap, so don't overwhelm yourself. Healing begets healing. You have plenty of time and grace to work on them at your own pace.

Heal the Hurt

Identify what hurts; identify the origin of the hurt. Is your self-esteem damaged? Begin there. Does it hurt that your relationships are limited in number and fulfillment? Is the hurt emotional, physical, mental? What does your toxic mother target with the purpose of hurting you or yours? Your reputation? Your confidence? Your finances? Your relationships? Are you depressed? Are you hurting others? Does your mother have a damaged soul from her own pain? This certainly was the case for mine. Sometimes, when we identify the hurt, we discover other things in our lives that won't let that hurt heal, most of which are also under our control.

Heal the Habits

Young sons of toxic mothers develop habits to survive with little awareness they are doing so. Young adults become ashamed of some of those habits and escape into their own rebellious or protective worlds.[34] The toxic environment seems to reinforce the habits, which serve as a means of relief or comfort for the son. This might include overeating, pornography, drinking, swearing, anger outbursts, workaholism, aloofness. It might show up in the form of Obsessive/Compulsive Disorder or overexercising, watching too much TV, hanging with the guys too much, or anything. Your job is to look honestly at your life and assess first what your habits are, even to the point of considering it addictive behavior. Then, you can decide whether those habits are healthy or do they negatively affect others, and, finally, does the negative effect of your habits generate toxic rules for you and others? Remember, these are <u>your</u> habits, not those of your mother. You cannot change her life, her routines, or her willingness to examine the impact she has on you. Heal *your* habits.

Heal the Heart (Learn to Love)

Examine your heart or motivation to love others, including your mother and yourself. A damaged heart has forgotten how or refuses to love. The pain is too much. Has your toxic mother's behavior toward you left you confused about how to love and be loved? Heal that! Begin with *Bold Love*[35] as described in this book. Whom do you want to love? Why haven't you? What do you believe about them or about love that has kept you from loving? Do you want to love your mother? Why or why not? Where does your heart go when your mother is persecuting you? Do you long to be away from your mother? Do you long to run toward her? Why or why not? There are as many healthy and unhealthy reasons to run away as there are to pursue her. What does your heart say? Do you even know? Why or why not?

For example, one of my reactions to my toxic mother was that I did not give myself permission to feel anything in the moment. My heart was beat into pulp where if I showed any emotion while my mother was stating her matriarchal declarations, she would tear into it to prove herself right about everything she deemed pathetic about my life. My mother would shame me, hit me, lie to me, withdraw from me, neglect me, manipulate me, and, I would close my heart to feel anything at all thinking my life would be better if I could get her to stop.

This occurred even into my adulthood. After leaving the scene of every train wreck interaction with my mother, I would stew on what she did and said and would rage at those around me—my own family. I needed to regain control of experiencing honest emotion in the precise moment I was experiencing it. Only then could I advocate for myself and choose the proper time and approach to maintain my own self-respect and integrity. As a by-product, doing it that way left me with little temptation to project my sadness, rage, and confusion onto my own family. I could love myself after my mom's abuse. I could "forgive" her in real time, not letting her sabotage the life I wanted to create. And, I could love my wife and kids. Heal your heart!

Heal with Heart (Jump in Joyfully)

As you heal, be proud of it! Heal <u>with</u> heart. Be zealous. There is nothing better than becoming the best you can be. Enlist your friends and family to be your cheerleaders. Find an accountability partner to check in on you to make sure you are making progress or to get you back on track. Celebrate and reward your progress, especially with those who love you well and whom you hope to love boldly too. Your heart will find joy when you restore everyone you choose to a better relationship with themselves, with God, or with others and even with you. Love recklessly those whom you choose to love and remember that you can forgive and you can ask for forgiveness. Relational conflict is inevitable, but any true, mature, healthy person can, with grace and humility, nurture their relationship with you if they hurt you or you them. There is freedom and grace to jump into life and relationships, and it's OK to expect to find joy and healing in the process.

After three miscarriages and thirteen years of marriage, it had become apparent that, more than our marriage, *I* needed help. As I worked with a therapist, we discovered how emotionless I was, and we worked hard on healing and nurturing my "inner child," who had been abused, neglected, and tossed aside to please my toxic mother. I did the work of therapy with all my heart. When I broke through and realized that my heart can begin feeling and trusting again, my therapist said, "Guy, go out and love your inner child" just like this book suggests in Figure 2, "and allow yourself to feel the joy and comfort of being loved." So, on my way I went.

I didn't really know what she meant, but I kept constantly seeking for an opportunity to let my inner child experience emotion. Ironically, it hit me when I walked into a Hardee's at lunch time. They were selling basketballs with every ACC logo on them. I bought one. Everyone who knows me knows I absolutely suck at ball sports. But, I took that basketball, asked them to fill it, left my car parked in the parking lot and bounced it all the way home . . . weeping at the joy of simple child's play. I was learning to let my heart feel. Let yours too.

Find Focus with Friendship

Whether you think you love your toxic mother or not, focus your preliminary healing efforts on those you know you do love. Practice loving them in a safer environment. Make friends with people of all kinds: acquaintances, interests, fellow classmates or training colleagues and more. Your newly-forming friendships will focus you to practice your new RTLB, and your focus will lead you to find a family of friends. Their love can help heal you, but focus on their health too.

Both love and loving really heal many wounds and scars. And, as described in this book, you might discover the toxic RTLB that you are imposing on your loved ones. Expand your family. Challenge yourself to love outside your comfort zone. And, if you can't think of anyone who is part of your family, or if you can't think of any healthy friendship circle you are a part of, you must ask yourself why. Recall the dangers of isolating or insulating yourself. Every son needs a focusing family of friends to love and that loves him. Your healing will be genuine as you heal in the midst of relationships. While loving boldly, heal your friendships, heal yourself!

My mentor, Ralph, discovered early on in our friendship that I had few friends who encouraged and whom I can encourage in the ways I was gifted. He challenged me to set goals, like rules-to-live-by, and to move out and make friends. I learned to ski and began to go on an annual trip with other men. I learned to play tennis. I became a Scout leader. And, then, Ralph challenged me to find better ways to love my new friends instead of demanding they read my mind and cater to me. So, I began to organize annual beach trips with men where I helped us form better friendships with ourselves while enjoying the beach the way only men can enjoy it. Food, fun, and focus. After every retreat, I have a new set of friends who know me and who have challenged me to continue my healing.

Heal Your Head (Mind Your Mind)

There are two ways to help you heal your head, both of which interact on some levels. The first "head" focus is to educate yourself. Learn something new, go to school, take a workshop, engage with others who are learning or doing something you believe to be of value. Learn what makes your head tick. Use personality tests, Enneagram,[36] and, my favorite, *StrengthsFinders 2.0.*[37] These measures help you understand the way you see the world, which helps you take in and enjoy more of the world. Learn the art of introspection. This sort of focus will suggest ways in which you can add value to whatever situation you choose to enter. The impact and accomplishments you achieve will energize you to continue growing and healing.

The second way to "heal your head" is with a mental health focus. Learn about mental health. Work on your own mental health. Learn how to live around and tolerate other people's mental health. My mother was toxic, she was delusional, she was a chronic liar, she was abusive to her children and husband, and I knew those around us—her friends, other family members, neighbors—were aware of her mental states. When my mother would spout her toxicity in public or become agitated when people would question her perception of reality, I would watch those nearby back down and simply nod. Many had submitted to her RTLB: "Don't challenge my mental capacity!"

I've spent enough time learning about mental illness that I now try to destigmatize it whenever I can. I speak about it naturally and publicly, in regular conversation. But, I also have worked on my own mental health. I struggle with anger management, I go through bouts of depression, or I withdraw from friends and family and rage at anyone who tries to bring me out of it. However, I seek professional help when I realize what is going on. I listen to others too when they tell me I'm unstable.

My daughter told me one New Year's Day resolution conversation that I needed to make new friends and rekindle the ones I already have. I agreed. It brought me out of a dark period of losing my sister, my father, my mother, and my brother, me having a heart attack, tearing my medial meniscus and Achilles tendon and more . . . all within a nine-year span. Grief too is a slippery slope and requires you to keep it in balance. Now, as a complete orphan, I am working through my grief. Heal your head. Learn something and care for your mental health.

Heal with Hope

Hope requires you to envision how things will look in the future. What do you want your healing to look like? How will you treat others, even your mother, when you have begun to heal? For healing from toxic mothers, hope usually implies waiting and looking for changes in our own thinking, beliefs, and behaviors that indicate we've established a new, more virtuous set of RTLB. Can you now interrupt your unhealthy mental and emotional patterns and remind yourself you are in control of your life now?

For me, I started out just hoping to make it through a family gathering. But, how will I know when I have made it through? So, hope in detail! Envision specific behavior or thought patterns you hope to adopt. Hope that those patterns come to mind subconsciously. As I did more of the work suggested in this book, I began to hope for more and for better. I wanted to be known for having virtues such as encouragement, generosity, humility, respect, kindness, love, service, gratitude, patience, and joy.

One way I chose to begin my healing was to put these virtues in my business plan. I have allotted time and resources for me to exercise generosity, service, and encouragement. I mentor young men and I pray for those whom I will be seeing and make a mental or written note about one thing I could say to encourage them. Always anticipating something better, I also know from growing in maturity that change takes time. Hope for the best, be anxious for nothing, but work like hell to make the changes you believe to be important and crucial to your healing. Don't despair when you make mistakes. There's always Grace. Hope for specific ways to heal.

Heal with Happiness (Conscious Contentedness)[38]

Don't worry, be happy! Is this the life philosophy on which we should hang our entire healing process? Probably not! But, there is psychological research backing a few principles that can help you heal from your toxic mother. First, consider what you believe being happy looks like and work on making that happen. Compare that to your current social, professional, or family relationships. Are you happy? Why or why not? What can you do to make yourself happy in each of those contexts? What do you enjoy? What do you do for entertainment? Does that entertainment invoke happiness in you? How does your toxic mother rob you of happiness? How can you find similar happiness without her attacks?

Second, help others be happy, it makes you happy too. What do your friends like to do? What do you like to do with friends?

Finally, be creative. Remember in Figure 2, you must step out into the field to play ball and find freedom from the imprisonment of your toxic mother. Here are two Hazel World stories that illustrate the role of happiness in my own healing. One may seem like a failure, but it was a smashing victory for me, attempting to make many happy but keeping my own happiness in mind as well. The other is more sentimental, but still chips away at my mother wound.

Bethany Beach

I was working on my happiness, and everyone knows the beach is my happy place. Within the span of a week I discovered Marie would be gone for a week, my brother loves Bethany Beach, and my mother was harassing me that she never gets to see my children—quite young at that time, Hope 3.5 years-old and Matthew, one year. My mother had also triangulated with me and my brother saying that Mark goes on all these family vacations and never brings his family to see her and that I "travel the world" but am embarrassed to go to see her in Pennsylvania. She was sobbing on the phone telling me that she can't even have a simple conversation with her grandchildren because they're so busy.

I despised being with my mother, incarcerated in the same house. She nagged me that I don't clean enough. She played the martyr that she always has to clean and no one else pitches in. I thought I would be creative and "love" my mother, so I picked the week Marie would be gone, rented two houses side by side in Bethany, invited my brother's whole family, my sister's too, and my parents. I was going to "solve" all of Mom's issues and "make her happy."

She immediately expressed horror about having to cook for everyone. She said she didn't have enough time (forty-five days) to prepare all the food at home so she could freeze it and carry it with her. No amount of my "pitching in" to clean, cook, or pay would ever satisfy her, and she lords that over me anyway until I end up watching her in an angry tirade narrate everything she's doing to keep everyone happy when, ironically, no one is happy around her. You get the picture. I kept trying, foolishly.

Solution? I told her I would pay for everything and I would bring the kids as long as she agreed to a few rules. First, she may not clean up; I had hired a maid service to come in daily. Second, she may not prepare food for any meal. I was providing *all* the food and beverages: breakfast and lunch foods we prepare on our own. And, we would go out to dinner for sure <u>every</u> evening where she would get to sit next to a chosen grandchild to enjoy them for the whole meal. I had secretly made reservations for several big lunches too. I traveled a day early to Delaware to prepare everything, from crib to grocery shopping to who's sleeping where.

I am not exaggerating that when my parents pulled up with my sister's family, frozen food came pouring out of the van. My mother jumped out, gathered up the food and "smiled."

"OK, Guy, show me where the freezers are. I've got everything here for our breakfast, lunch, and dinner."

I immediately felt the rage in my veins. Next, she brought out a broom and dustpan.

"You know how much the kids track in sand. I'm going to have to sweep every five minutes to keep the sand out of the houses."

This time I "smiled."

"Gee, Mom, I thought it was clear I was taking us out to dinner because you wanted to have one-on-one time with the grandchildren and you didn't want to cook. What's all this?"

"Guy, you always think money is the solution to everything. We can't afford to go out for every meal."

I thought, "Maybe you can't afford it, but I can afford it for everybody."

What I said, however, was victorious.

"OK, but I'm not sticking around the chaos when we all don't fit into one house and you get all anxious about cooking and cleaning. And I'll walk out to the beach if I hear you bitchin' about how much you have to do. I offered for you to have a true vacation, and this stuff just tells me you don't want my generosity. I thought you'd be happy to have no responsibilities and lots of time to love on your grandchildren."

My mother snapped at me that I had no right assuming the reasons she brought the food, and I just smiled and said, "OK, I'm sure you have your reasons too."

When my dad observed this interaction, he let me know two things.

"Guy, I never knew you wanted to do that. Your mother never told me." And, "I like the idea, so I'm going to take you up on at least a couple of those dinners. We can haul the frozen food back home with us."

I stayed true to my word. I took us out when my father advocated, and I walked away and never cleaned or cooked. I was entitled to my own happiness. The beach is where it's at! I remained happy even when failing at making my mother happy.

The Grand Ole Opry

I suspected my mother's cancer had metastasized the moment she found out, and I repeatedly asked her bluntly if it was true. She lied. She constantly begged me to leave my home in North Carolina, fly to Tucson, Arizona and "help" her. She cried on the phone that her blindness was keeping her from enjoying traveling. Most everything she said or did was twisted with her toxic manipulation.

For example, when she found out I would not be going to Arizona at her beck and call because my family came first, she said in a sweet voice, "Well, Guy, you are such a great dad to spend so much time with your kids. No one I know has traveled with their kids as much as you. You get to do that because you and Marie have money! THAT'S why you don't have time to come here!"

I replied simply, "Well, I'm glad my work lets me have the flexibility. I've worked hard to get myself in that position."

My mother started crying again saying her Arizona friend, Kathy, was going on a trip through Nashville, "because she's rich, and she's going to visit a rich friend." They were going to visit the Noah's Ark replica. I let go of my anger and her toxic insults to my character and decided to combine my efforts to make her happy while helping me find a bit of happiness, myself.

I simply said, "Mom, I have an idea. Ask Kathy if you can go with her. I'm sure you can overcome the blindness obstacles with Kathy's help. I've seen you two do it before. I'll pay for your ticket and pay for all three of you to stay in a hotel in Nashville the first night and I'll take you all to the Grand Ole Opry," a dream of hers since I can remember. "I'll fly to Nashville, see you guys for the performance and then visit Matthew (my son in college in Nashville)."

Of course, she started with, "Oh, Guy, you and Kathy are rich and you can just make plans like that, but I can't do that? And Kathy has already asked me to go, but I told her I just can't afford it."

"Well, Mom, it'll be your loss. You'd get to see a performance at your dream venue, eat with me, and see Matthew while you get to travel with the help you need to get around."

Remember, I still don't know she is terminally ill. This is just a simple manipulation about wealth and blindness.

Has Mom manipulated me into coughing up a plane fare and a show I know she *can* afford? In fact, I had been telling her to spend her money and stop trying to save it for her "legacy." It wasn't much money. None of that mattered. I hung up on my mother.

"Mom, I'll call you right back."

I called Kathy, asked her if my mother could go. She immediately said yes. I offered to pay for their hotel room in Nashville. I booked one for the three women and one for me, bought Mom's plane ticket, and dinner and a Christmas show at the Ryman Theatre for all four of us.

The trip brought Mom much joy, and it also continued my journey to learn to love my mother boldly. Specifically, I had really learned to state truth to her, let it fall on her ears, let her react in her own toxic way, and then do what I knew would restore her to better relationship with herself, others, and God. She loosened up a bit and enjoyed traveling like she used to. She bonded with Kathy and her friend well. She took that time to be happy with my son, enough that she felt comfortable telling us both the "truth" that her cancer was spreading and she had very limited time left in this life. She told me she was at peace with God, she was refusing treatment, she was glad she could tell Matthew in person since he was her "most sensitive" grandchild (don't even try to unpack that). Armed with a good set of RTLB, having practiced baby steps of loving my mother boldly, our relationship began a faster-paced restoration where I was free to be myself, speak my truth, live with her warped sense of it, and enjoy being with her during her last six months. I am forever grateful.

Heal with Humor

Look for the humor in the demands of your toxic mother's RTLB. Find a way to humor your mom by letting her know you are aware of her game/demands and that you can respect them to a certain point, but in your world, you find the demand funny.

As you get better at creating virtuous RTLB, you will also be able to detect your mother's BS and demands. When you detect the BS, there is usually a toxic, or at least illogical, demand to accompany it. Don't be afraid to see the humor—or absurdity—of the demand. And, when you see that humor, you will immediately experience less intensity in the baggage of the demand. You can tolerate it yourself more easily, and she will be stripped of her expectations to control, sabotage, gaslight, and humiliate. Expose it as humor. Humor is funny because there is an element of truth embedded in it. Drive the truth as humor. Laugh, and try to laugh with your mother. Be honest with her, but laugh when you see the humor.

BS Meter

I had planned to stay with my mother every other week beginning in January and staying with her full time when hospice told me to. Those were my boundaries, and my mother agreed. Every week while at my home, I would get a call. Mom would sound like she was too feeble to put a fork to her mouth. At first, I went flying back to Tucson sooner than I had planned, with a more expensive ticket and with the lengthy trip itself taking its toll on my physical health. When I arrived, Mom sounded "distressed" for about 1.5 seconds. She would show me all the food she'd prepared for me. She had plans for us to go to shows in her retirement community. She had a list of friends she wanted to visit to "show me off." The transformation was incredible.

Gently but frankly, I told my mother that I didn't understand when she demanded to have her great life of independence in Arizona, to which I accommodated, but at the same time, she would sound terrible on the phone, making me rush out there and interrupt <u>my</u> life. This happened over and over again, and the stress was weighing on me and my family. When my mother finally decided to call hospice, I sat down with our hospice nurse (Katy) in my mother's presence and said:

"Katy, I need a bull$hit meter. You know, like a gauge that goes from left to right. Left is complete BS and right is an accurate perception of her health and need for my assistance. According to Mom, she is not quite in the stage of dying where she needs full-time care, but when I call, it sounds like she's minutes from death. And, when I get here, she resurrects and makes me cookies, my favorite meal, and more. I need you, Katy, to be able to give me your 'professional measurement' of her BS on this scale whenever I ask you. I don't trust her to tell me, and I have to live my life too. So, let's begin right now. In your opinion, how accurately do you think Mom is reporting her condition and symptoms."

The whole time, I used my hand and finger to indicate the arrow on the BS dial.

"Is it a zero on the BS scale? Is it a 20 percent?"

I looked over at my mom and her face was between the "how-dare-you" glare and bursting into laughter. I didn't care which! I thought it was funny. Katy did too.

Mom laughed, and Katy said simply, "Twenty out of 100! And, since you are on Hazel's HIPAA forms, I can tell you that figure whenever you call."

No One Must Know!

Since laughter sometimes is the only medicine to healing from toxic mothers, I must share another story. My mother insisted that NO ONE knew of her terminal illness. Absolutely no one. I thought it was a stupid idea. It put undue pressure on me to make excuses about why I was constantly visiting my mother. I got to know many of her friends, none of which knew my mother's fate. In fact, my mother shared a trash bin with her next-door neighbor, Phyllis. I truly had to knock on her door to say, "Hi, Phyllis, Mom is dead and I need your garbage bin." My mother threw herself a "goodbye" party with her friends and family, but insisted on no one knowing her condition. Awkward! But I obliged.

My Path to Acceptance: Some Background

Back to the real story! I'm stepping off a plane to visit my mother, who has been given one month to live. My sister—already dead. My father—already dead. My mother—having already shacked up with and become engaged to the most repulsive substitute for my father, that fiancé—dead from lung cancer. I'm exhausted from the early flight totaling nine hours of travel. My mother has told me we'll be going out to dinner as soon as I arrive. And all I could do is rage in my head that I may not tell anyone of her impending death.

Why the angst? Well, how will I act when all she's worried about is that her friends might find out she's terminally ill. How do I live *this* pretense when I've spent my entire adult life escaping her Hazel World and ridding myself of the very lies she beat into me . . . verbally, emotionally, and physically? How do I rid myself of any pretense? How do I know my reflection and healing have led me down a DIFFERENT path to make the RIGHT decisions to honor her, to love her, to restore her relationship with my only remaining brother, with me, and with God? How do I know I am accomplishing my goals to live my life free from her? How do I love her well and apply the principles I hold so personally and so hopefully to the real-world task of helping my mother die a dignified death, the one she has burnt into her brain, the one she is insisting will transpire the exact way she imagines? How will I know my plan is working . . . that plan to maintain my integrity and heal from her craziness? I want to be in control of how I choose to care best for my mother.

The Plan

Her decline was happening faster now. But so was her demand that no one know. I was depleting my supply of RTLB to handle the situations that surfaced too often. My plan for this visit was first and simply to tell her <u>my</u> truth . . . <u>my</u> truths . . . my promises to myself. Here are some:

- It's hard for me to live the lie that she's not dying, but I'll do it for her.

- I will honor her wishes as much as I can, but I can't read her mind and I'll not be treated poorly when I haven't. She must be forthright about what she wants and needs.

- I'm going to be real about everything. I will never lie to her. I will tell her my truth, but she may not demand I accept hers. God is big enough to handle the mismatch.

- Even though she believes I should have visited much more than I ever did, she can trust me to be here for her in her everyday life and I can help her be comfortable with her new normal each biweekly visit until she becomes bed-ridden.

- I can take care of her and myself; she is not to feel obligated or guilty about her difficulty in caring for herself or me. She has taught me well how to do both. These circumstances are new to us both, so we must both speak up when we are discussing the future.

- She does not owe me anything. She does not need to leave me with any material thing.

- I forgive her for anything she may have perpetrated against me and do not hold grudges. I hope she can do the same for me. I'm willing to talk about any related issues, but correct blame is <u>not</u> the goal.

- My life is my life, and I am responsible to live it the way I believe to be proper, godly, honorable, honoring and responsible. When she is dead, it will not matter to her, anyway. Being with Jesus will be so much more important than whether I have a memorial for her against her wishes or I "boo-hoo" over her passing.

The Hilarious Point of Acceptance

A lot is at stake here. I want to "debut" my new attitude. We have lots to discuss, lots to process, but I was committed to being present and engaged for my mother. She wanted to eat out with her friends. I obliged.

From the airport and to her house to pick her up, we don't delay leaving for the steak house. We arrive early, but not as early as the fuddy-duddies at the "over 55" community where she owns a small two-bedroom home she keeps impeccably organized to facilitate her movement . . . due to her blindness. The club meets at a new restaurant each Friday at 5 p.m. We arrived at 4:30 and were the last ones to arrive. Hence, we were "stuck" sitting alone at our own table.

We order, we chat, and I ask her about her friends sitting at nearby tables. As she describes each, she shouts their names for them to look over and wave. "Kathy? Darwin? Patty?" Mind you, she can't see them, but she wanted to show me off. I return the waves and smile politely.

"Vince?" Picture the worst stereotype of a mafioso, grey-headed, greased-back coif of swag with macho gold chains and a t-shirt with a V-neck that goes lower than his beltline.

He begins to approach, so I say, "Mom, who's that? He reminds me of Franki Vali meets the Godfather."

"Oh, Guy. That's Vince. He's sweet on me. Is he coming here?"

"Yep!" And, with a sheepish grin only she could hear, I whisper, "And . . . Are you OK with this? With *him*? . . . Mom, does he know about your cancer? He's coming this way!"

"No, he doesn't know. No one here but Kathy knows about my diagnosis. No one else must know! He's alright, but he's a bit cheesy! I don't know what to do about him."

I sat for an eternity and, thankfully it was also an eternity for an old man to get out of his seat and amble his way toward us, especially with his flirtatious jingle of strutting sexy! Then, before he was in hearing range, I lean over and say in my mother's ear, "Well, if he's sweet on YOU, he better UP his game. He hasn't got that much time!"

My mother howled with laughter. I did too. We look up at poor Vince.

"Nice to meet you, Vince," but he was only interested in why we were laughing. We couldn't regain our composure, but I broke into more formalities. "Where are you from, Vince?" et cetera. Of course, it was awkward. Nothing could have convinced Vince we were not using him as the butt of many, many socially inappropriate jokes.

"Oh, Vince. It's totally an inside joke. Way too much context to bring anyone on board. Do you want to sit with us? Mom isn't eating, but I ordered the pizza, and you can share."

Dejected and not even knowing why, Vince declined and huffed back to his original seat.

It was then that I knew. I could leave the baggage at the airport. Humor had led me to acceptance. I had designed an appropriate set of RTLB so that I could enter Hazel World and be unscathed by her toxicity. They were also RTLB to help me love, cherish, and honor my mother. I could ignore my selfish, internal demands for retribution from a woman who I felt crushed and abandoned me. I could set aside the stupidity of playing the charade that my mother was not dying. My new RTLB allowed oxygen to flow, bringing joy to my mother in her saddest and most vulnerable times. Even to the point of laughing at the depravity of the situation.

Heal with Hands Open

The road to healing is not a straight line. It has bumps and curves that might discourage us from staying on the path. It takes work and patience to love boldly, seemingly fail, and get up and try it again. Healing with your hands open is a symbolic gesture to remind you of a few things about your attempts at healing from a toxic mother. First, it's a lifetime journey, not a one-time fix. Second, the open hands signify a humility that you can't do this by yourself. You need something or someone else to help you through. Next, the hands are "open" and relaxed, not clench-fisted. As we create our new RTLB, as we see the importance of developing character and virtues to make ourselves better and place ourselves in a position to heal and love, we run the risk of holding onto our rules tightly and throwing them bluntly at others. We want to control and impose our RTLB onto others when we, ourselves, can't or don't even follow the same rules. A hand with palm up cannot judge or hit. Finally, we open our hands to give somebody something we have. The open hand faces upward as if we are giving to or receiving from a higher power. Give the guilt and shame to God. Receive the Grace and healing from God. Release the power your toxic mother has over your life. Give yourself the freedom to love boldly and receive the forgiveness when you fall short. The open hand indicates how you must work to have and maintain a proper mindset when working on issues so volatile.[39]

An adaptation of Matthew 7:7 provides structure to three categories of strategies you can use while you focus on healing from your toxic mother.

> [7] "Ask and it will be given to you; seek and you will find; knock and the door will be opened to you."

In order to take charge of your healing, especially from your toxic mother, consider these twists on the three commands: ASK . . . SEEK . . . KNOCK . . . .

CHAPTER 10

ASK, BUT GIVE IN RETURN

When attempting to heal from toxic mothers, we sons must first do the work of taking charge of our own life, our own virtue, our own courage to step into the world and do things differently. As your confidence grows in the process, there will come a crossroads in your journey where you choose whether to approach your mother for any reason. Communicating with a toxic mother or anyone assumes the risk that you will be asking for something from that person. With your newfound RTLB, speak freely to your mother, but remember, the only thing you can control is what you say and what you do. So, ask your mother for something, perhaps expecting some sort of reply. Plan what you would like to say and how based on your own RTLB, including maintaining your own health and integrity. In addition, plan what you would be willing to give even if she does not respond like a rational mother ought.

What follows are important items or scenarios in which you might want to discuss a topic with your mother during your healing. Ask, knowing you have done the work to survive and even thrive no matter her response. One way to remind yourself that you control your life now is to acknowledge that you are . . . or are **not** . . . willing to give something up when your toxic mother turns your request to her into an attack at your most vulnerable places. If you are indeed healing, you will have welcomed a support team of people into your life and your world—people who love you and whom you love boldly. You will have developed yourself to live the way you choose, and you will still have a world intact in which you can practice developing virtue and character such as being generous, helpful, or encouraging, all the while enjoying the fruits of your work both in your own heart and with others. The following two RTLB frame the rest in this category to "ask, but give in return."

> 1. Ask your mother for what you want and need, but expect her to deflect and ask the same from you.

Don't ask your toxic mother for anything you are unwilling to provide yourself. You need your mother to know what you need from her. Give her the Grace to turn it around and ask you for the same. I'm sure you will have heard it before: it's always about her and not about you! Even if your requests are empty words to her as hers probably are to you, now you know she knows. What she probably is not expecting is that you can walk away from that conversation sad but intact, confident and proactive to move on and keep on healing. Congratulations!

> 2. Ask her to tell you specifically what she wants and needs, but provide for her on your terms.

You get to decide what you give to your mother whether she asks for it or not. Ask her to be clear and specific with her requests and demands. Then, speak to her about what you are willing to do and give. You do not have to tell her about her double standards of not giving you what you ask for while she demands you cater to her whims. Set the stage yourself by laying down your RTLB: "Even though someone asks me to do something, I am not obligated. In fact, I deserve the respect enough to discuss exactly what terms I will use to respond to the request."

After setting down the rule that she be clear with what she wants, feel the freedom either to say no with no justification or to reply with a return request for her to clarify the demand. Provide her what you agreed on with no expectations of her gratitude or her changed behavior or personality. This RTLB requires discipline and trustworthiness.

There were many times I second-guessed giving my mother what I said I would. I overthought how she could use it against me yet again, or how I now didn't simply want to punish her for her horrible treatment. Deliver what you promise. My wife has even taught me to UNDERpromise and OVERdeliver. I recommend it. As you move on, you will discover creativity to negotiate with and provide for your toxic mother. Here are some examples of specific things to ask for and things to give her for the greater good of *your* healing and moving on.

1. Ask for patience, but give her the break.

If you are old like I am, you probably remember the bumper stickers with the cute cat saying, "Have patience with me. God isn't finished with me yet." I can tell you from experience that asking God and others for patience with me was so much easier than asking my mother. There may come a time when your mother is impatient with you. Feel the freedom to ask her for patience. Feel free to ask God to give her patience or to give you patience with her. Work on your patience with others in your safer zones of healing. But, when it is all said and done, give your mom a break. The anger and bitterness will eat you alive. You do not need her acceptance or patience for you to conform to her whim how she would like . . . ever! You are loved and accepted exactly as you are, no matter how you choose to handle your life circumstances. Give her a break and ask your higher power for the ability to do so. You can move on much easier when you do not hold grudges or make yourself beholden to your toxic mother.

2. Ask for appropriate things but be generous with/to all.

I rarely asked my mother for anything. Remember when I asked her to babysit my children at my house? I cannot tell you how much bitterness I stuff down when I recount that story. But, I chose to "be generous in all things." When I got home, I called my wife in Germany to rage, and she simply went into "Marie-mode!" She problem-solved who could babysit when, where I could do my work in peace, and even how I would eat. She is the love of my life!

I shared my story with Ralph, my mentor. His first response was, "I thought you did this trip to give your mother the time she demanded to be with your children? Your parents chose returning a leaf blower instead of being with you and your kids?" But, Ralph, although he could not hide his dismay and unbelief regarding my life, kept a healthy, godly demeanor. He immediately reminded me to "be generous." That was a goal I was working on. So . . . I bought my parents a leaf blower and had it delivered to their house. YES, there was a hint of spite and revenge. But, I was being generous too. God can handle my mixed motives. I'm just trying to move on with my own life. I can't be anchored down by the $hit coming at me from my toxic mother.

3. Ask for forgiveness, but give it in return.

Jesus said, "Turn the other cheek." And, I had had lots of experience with that as I switched cheeks from being spanked with a hairbrush handle. Frankly, I had had enough turning of my cheeks. But, I had to relearn how to ask for forgiveness.[40] I can only control my own life, and I had inflicted harm to my mother simply by my anger and avoidance. I have learned through many life experiences and in Christian counseling that I need to ask my mother for forgiveness for those things brought to my attention. However, my forgiveness is not dependent on whether my mother forgives me. I am not required to be forgiven by my mother, but I am obligated to attempt to love her boldly. God loves me whether I love well or not. My asking her for forgiveness is a small part of how I can try to restore her to a better relationship with me, with herself, with others, and with God. Asking for forgiveness may restore the other person or not, but it frees me to continue my goals for virtue and integrity.

I do not ask for forgiveness in order to manipulate my mother to ask me for the same. If I want to develop humility, I cannot exercise control or have unrealistic expectations that she will reciprocate and ask me to forgive her. I can only work on growing in character and healing myself.

I am also called to forgive. And so are you. Forgive your mother even if she doesn't ask for it. Examine your own understanding of Grace, forgiveness, grudges, and related issues. My understanding of the role of forgiveness in my life needed some clarification, most of which I acquired in counseling and with trusted, mature friends who accepted my apologies as much and as well as they apologized.

I needed flesh and blood experiences to move on from horrible experiences.

Me? Apologize? Are You Kidding?

After the guilt and judgment my mother hurled at me and my family, I finally agreed my wife and kids and I would accompany my parents on a getaway trip with some of their friends and those friends' children. When we arrived at the "condo" the sleeping arrangements were tight. My mother had already decided our one-year-old son would be sleeping in a crib in a separate room with their friend's son. I had met him before. He would stay with my parents in their extra room while he was in town. His parents did not live in Lancaster anymore. I said that was OK, so we started to set up. Unfortunately, the fold-out crib didn't fit in the boys' room, so Marie and I stuffed it into our cramped room and we and our children all slept in one room. Even though it was a short stay, we ran out of diapers quickly and simply went out to buy more. The trip was as fun as could be with a toxic mother who attempted to control everyone's interaction while judging those who were not in her presence.

Six years later, my father accidentally let it slip that the boy in whose room my mother tried to force my son's crib had a diaper fetish. He would buy diapers, put them on himself and his cousins and "play" until sexually aroused. I hung up on my dad and told him I would call him right back. When I called back, I could tell my mother knew what was coming. Not surprising and in typical oppressive, controlling fashion, she took the phone from my father.

I raged, "How long ago did you know about this."

"Well, Guy, don't get upset. We've known about it for a really long time. He's trying to work on it more right now."

"So, you KNEW he was struggling with this $hit and you were trying to put Matthew in the same room with him? Is that why we ran out of diapers?"

"Well, probably. We learned that he was playing with the diapers with the other children on the trip. Those were probably Matthew's."

I couldn't process it quickly enough. My son was saved only because his crib didn't fit in this kid's room. Could our daughter have been affected by this? I had to think about when and where and with whom she was playing during that vacation. I was pretty sure she was safe. But, then, I started sobbing.

"Mom, the only reason I can say with certainty that Matthew was OK was that he DIDN'T fit into that kid's room. YOU kept trying to find ways to put him there! Why would you do that?"

Silence!

"MOM, do you have anything to say to that?"

Silence!

"Well, I can tell you I am never going to bring my family to stay there again! I can't trust you! I've stayed there with my kids at the same time when he was staying there. You guys can come down here whenever you want, but there's no way I'm going to let you have my children in Pennsylvania by yourself ever. You've been asking for me to send them up to stay with you *by themselves*? Do you think I could ever trust you now that this has happened?"

"Guy, I thought you were a Christian. You're supposed to forgive kids like that and you're supposed to forgive and love your mother. You're being irrational and it's affecting your religion."

WHAT IS THAT SUPPOSED TO MEAN? It certainly wasn't an apology.

After reviewing my RLTB, knowing I can only ask for forgiveness and forgive, I called my mother and apologized for my "overreaction." I was sorry for yelling. She began to lay in to me again.

"You're darn right you need to ask for forgiveness. I'm your mother!"

"Well, Mom, I wasn't done yet. I also want to say I forgive **you** for what you did to put our son in danger. But I still am going to hold my ground. I will never go to Pennsylvania to stay with you again. I may go there to visit but we will stay where we want. You guys are welcome to come here and see the kids whenever you want, and Marie and I will pay your way to stay somewhere else.

"Well, Guy, that's not forgiveness, that's punishment!"

"No, Mom, this is me taking responsibility for my children's safety, and you are not safe to be with my kids alone."

"I'm sorry you feel that way." This was no apology.

"I'm not! My family comes first, and it takes complete priority over you, your ideas of being a Christian, over whether you think I'm punishing you!"

I had to work hard at purging myself of the inappropriate and inaccurate information and RTLB about how I wanted to live my life loving boldly, healing unselfishly, and moving on. I'm glad I had done some of that work before this scenario occurred. I needed an apology, but I forgave instead.

4. Ask for respect but give her space and time.

You don't need your toxic mother's respect, but you can ask her for it. At the very least, your asking indicates you are taking charge of your own life and moving on, with or without it. Make sure when you ask for it that you know exactly what you mean and want regarding how she should respect you. Use that as your standard. If she is as toxic as you think, she will observe how you are actively turning yourself into a man of character, respect, dignity, ethics, love, and more. And, if your mother is like mine, if you ask her for respect, she'll probably remind you that you don't respect her and that she is way more deserving of your respect than you are of hers. Ask anyway! Give her the time and space to process your request, expect nothing, and, during that time, *work on you.*

5. Ask for truth, but give her Grace.

In life with a toxic mother, truth and lies come in many and similar packages. A toxic mother usually deals in lies of multiple natures. She distorts the truth. She keeps truth from you. She lies to tell you what she believes you should know or want to hear. Let's face it. Your healing would come much more completely if she told you the truth, but, when you ask her for it, she draws back her bow and arrow for the kill. She assumes your request for the truth demonstrates you are vulnerable and confused. Mom hardly ever told my siblings and me the truth. It was tainted or filtered through a lens that we would spend days, years, or decades trying to decipher. Here's a case in point.

Where have you been? What is that?

My mother has a scar from her pubic hairline to between her breasts. When I was thirteen years old, my mother disappeared for three days. My father was working lots (or shacking up lots, I'm still not sure), but when she got home all three of us kids asked her why she had stitches. She just smiled and said, "Oh, they did exploratory." Remember, I was thirteen years old. I am currently fifty-eight. In the last weeks of her conscious life, her friend asked her what the scar was from and she said, "Oh, they did exploratory." From her surgery date until her death, forty-five years, I asked her at least once a year why she had that scar, what were they "exploring," and she never told me. I'm left wondering why she didn't trust me to tell me the truth at any time in our relationship.

That "truth" is none of my business

As another illustration of how truth can be used as a toxic device to control others consider my mother's journey with her fiancée. She can spew venom or truth, and at times they are the same, but my job is to give her grace but let her know I work on truth. How she draws others into Hazel World is not my responsibility. Roy became smitten with my mother when she moved part-time to Arizona to be closer to the weather and her sisters. They got engaged—ring and all. She was like a giddy teenager for a few weeks. It was weird, but I was glad widow and widower alike had found love.

But, as my mother became blinder, she constantly complained that her fiancée was introverted and anti-social. She said he did not want to get married, so they cohabitated. I knew she was manipulating him, but I had no reason to doubt these "truths." But the facts never added up. He played tennis and pickle ball with the most intense man who is now my friend, Mr. Dan Bennett. Roy would tell me stories of how he hunted, hung out with his friends, camped, and did other social activity. He was quite sterile while describing how their joint home was put into a trust because they were not married. It didn't add up, but I didn't care.

Mom's "truths" never came at me unless they served to advance her lie, however. After I repeated these "truths" to Dan, Roy's best friend in Arizona, he quickly informed me that Roy felt suffocated by my mother. She would not marry him even though he wanted to. Roy wanted to play more tennis and go off with his friends, but she would drag him to her "fun band" or "dress-up parties" which Roy consistently told me, personally, he hated.

Don't get me wrong. I knew my place in this relationship. I didn't want to know the truth. It was none of my business what their arrangements were, and I consistently told them that. While I was in the middle of processing all that, I invited Mom and Roy to our home while they were romping and shagging across America in his camper-truck. I, of course, "surprised" them with a hotel stay in a historic hotel in Winston-Salem, safely avoiding my mother's criticism of how I keep house and the awkwardness of putting them in the same room and bed in my own house. One afternoon, my mother came with that Hazel World look of glazed eyes, and I knew the conversation would go south momentarily.

"Guy, now you know Roy and I are married in God's eyes. We are only deciding to live together because of our retirement. And, Roy has a lot of money and wants to make sure it goes to his children. He doesn't want to get married. I have to know—do you think I'm a slut for staying with him?

"Mom, that's none of my business. You are old enough you can make that decision, and you should not be thinking about other people's opinions. Make that judgment yourself. Isn't that what you taught me?" I thought if I turned her toxic RTLB back at her, she would have nowhere to go.

"So, you DO think I'm a prostitute. You DON'T agree with how Roy and I are traveling around in his truck!"

"Mom, I didn't come anywhere close to saying that. It looks like to me you're feeling guilty because you decided not to marry Roy." I was really testing the "truth" she had been telling me. I challenged it straight on.

Instantly, she asserted, "I've always wanted to get married. It's Roy who doesn't. You think I'm a whore, don't you?"

"Mom, I'm not having this conversation unless you want to bring Roy right in here with us to hear what I think. It is not my call! You guys can and should do exactly what you want. I have no right to tell you what to do. I want to hear what Roy has to say. Shall I go get him?"

"No, no! I wanted to know how you felt about us being together."

"Mom, all I heard was you trying to get me to free you of the guilt you may be experiencing. I can't help you with that no matter what my opinion is. I think you and Roy can figure it out, especially if you love each other like you say. I'm done with this conversation." This preserved the integrity of my RTLB to be honest and truthful only while restoring people to a better relationship with themselves, me, others or their God.

I didn't "ask" Mom for truth, but I certainly tested its accuracy. And I gave her Grace. I really did believe she was trying to absolve herself of the guilt for shacking up with a dude over a candy bar. (It's a long story.) I offered her the Grace to explore her guilt freely and non-judgmentally, whether she confessed, told me "another" truth, broke up with the dude, or became his concubine.

Before understanding how to give Grace, I would rage when I caught her in a lie. She would rage back, and then she would confess and bring up the same old scenario. She was a victim, I was judgmental, I couldn't handle the truth, I didn't know what I was talking about, her father made her fear telling the truth, blah, blah, blah. I thought I had exercised healthy boundaries and restored her to a better understanding of my unconditional love for her.

That Wasn't Enough

I thought I had done a terrific job asking her for truth and giving her Grace, but I had made too many assumptions that Mom had been restored to a better relationship with anyone (Roy, herself, others, or God). I believed that after our prior interaction, she had reconciled her cohabitating escapades in her own heart. I was trusting too much in the idea that I had moved on too. I obviously was not ready to be blindsided.

A month later, I had bought my mom the same great phone that I had because it had terrific accessibilities for blindness. We had planned for me to visit for a week and for me to teach her how to use Uber, how to use the accessibility functions, and more. It turned out that Roy had contracted lung cancer and was dying, and I didn't want her to be alone without the ability to go out or grocery shop or reach me, or do normal life activities. When I arrived, Roy was sick from his chemotherapy. He squirted diarrhea all over his favorite and only chair in which he stayed. I maturely told my mother to bathe him and I would clean up the mess. Mom came outside with an angry voice and said, "Guy, why would you choose to clean up Roy's diarrhea when you think he's taking advantage of me."

"What do you mean?"

"Well, you think we're just shacking up living in sin, but you're cleaning up his mess."

And, then it struck me! She had *not* responded at all to my Grace. She needed more! "Mom, even if I thought Roy was taking advantage of you, I'm trying to learn not to hold grudges. You both are adults and can do what you want. As for Roy, he needs help, and I can do that. Why wouldn't I help? I'm not punishing you for being with Roy by cleaning up his diarrhea. Do you see how ridiculous that is?" Here is a truth I was able to articulate at the very moment I needed it.

She was still angry, probably because I had exposed her lie with a truth. "You're just rubbing it in to say I told you so."

"Mom, you're getting out of control. Stop going down the rabbit hole of shame and guilt and blame and punishment. I'm in Arizona to help you, but Roy needs help more. I truly don't care about Roy, but you do. So, I'm helping you now with Roy hoping that I can help you learn how to use your phone later."

"You don't care about Roy?"

"No. I don't like him. He's not Dad. That's not his fault, it's my issue. I'm not cleaning up his diarrhea to rub it in that I'm right. That's your issue. I don't think you trust that I'm mature enough to do the right thing by helping you clean up after Roy even though he's shacking up with you. I've got the diarrhea cleanup. You just make sure Roy's OK and stop pushing your $hit onto me!"

She turned around and walked into their bedroom.

6. Ask for Grace, but give her Truth.

Every time I went to my mother to confess how I had wronged

her, I was asking for her Grace. She snapped at the opportunity to drive her darts deeper into my heart. My only defense was to calmly reply with the truth. When you try to love your toxic mother boldly and it turns south, give yourself Grace first. At least you are trying to love or apologize. But, when she is lambasting you into the ground, you have every right to walk away. At least stand on the truth. Know the truth. Remember that when you apologize to a healthy person, he will welcome your attempt to restore relationship. That's what grownups do.

While bedridden during the last four weeks of her life, Mom and I were able to talk about a lot of things. We both made regular baby steps toward loving each other boldly. There were sweet, tender moments of normalcy. During one conversation, however, I reacted pretty explosively to my mother's confession that she had kept me from hanging out with my best high school friend, Barry Goldman. I was inappropriately angry. I felt as though she had stripped me of one of the few things that brought me joy in my childhood. Was she shameless? Can she not exercise the smallest amount of grace that sometimes it is *not* about her? Does she have any ability to know how her RTLB have affected me? I was demanding the grace for her to have treated me with the dignity and kindness that might have nourished my soul at a very vulnerable time in the life of my family of origin. But, I raged at her. I walked out of the house without my phone on purpose. I wanted to punish her. She was sick, blind, and dying, and I didn't care if she needed my help then. I didn't want to hear truth from anyone, especially her.

After realizing how I had hurt my mother, I approached her to apologize. She returned it with, "He wasn't good for you, anyway. He was rich. He could never be your friend. I didn't keep you from him. I just tried to limit your time with him." She just spouted off lies and generalizations all derived from her toxic rules-to-live-by.

I said calmly, "Mom, he was the kindest person to me in high school. He introduced me to great people, great ideas, and great habits like taking care of a car, like how to hold your tongue when someone was being a jerk, like how to love your father even though he's a nut! If you don't think those things were good things for me to receive from a friend who accepted your son for who he was, then you don't understand why I was so angry when I found that out. I can't change the past, and I'd love to catch back up with Barry one day. I was wrong to be so verbally abusive to you. I'm sorry. I needed you to understand my perspective, but it doesn't make my outburst right. Again, I'm sorry."

After a moment of silence, I went to bed. I felt like I had relapsed and needed the Grace of my God's forgiveness since my apology had fallen on toxic ears. I had regressed two steps and needed to start moving on from the setback. I remembered my gratitude for my friendship with Barry at such a formative time for me and fell asleep ready to step into the toxic arena the next day, equipped with a newer, more refined set of RTLB.

7. Ask to be mentored, but mentor younger men

This sounds easier than it is. Men don't seek a formal relationship with other men except when there is a pretense. That pretense could be romantic, professional such as in executive coaching, or athletic such as a trainer. But very few men know how to mentor and even fewer advertise that they do. I'm not talking about a paid mentor, although that would be more like a therapist or counselor or life coach. To complicate things, very few men are encouraged to seek counseling, let alone to look for a mentor. Let's look at both sides of this coin: to mentor or be mentored.

Searching for Mentors: Kicking the Tires, Lifting the Hood, and Taking a Test Drive

When I find I'm stuck in any part of my healing, I try to assess what I would need to move on from that obstacle. Then, I look for men usually with more age but definitely with more expertise, experience, wisdom, integrity, and personability. These men listen well, are not presumptuous, and are growing the ways you are hoping to. They are outspoken about their need to heal, particularly from their toxic mothers. They are further along the healing journey than you. They are someone like my mentor, Ralph. Because they reveal their brokenness, look at them like an old, classic car.

Look from afar and make sure you experience any deal-breaking incompatibility. When you see what you like, do your research on that "car." What do they do? Whom do they employ or who employs them? Does their story embrace the healing work you are doing? What are his RTLB? Then, kick his tires! Introduce yourself to him. Attend an event that he attends or leads. Send him an email and introduce your goals for healing. Then, lift up the hood and look. Ask if you can meet with him to discuss his journey dealing with his toxic mother. See if the engine revs at the prospect. Then, take a test-drive! Ask if he will meet with you once or twice to see if he would be interested in helping you work through some sticky situations with your mother. If he runs well and you like the ride, then "buy it!" Go after it with gusto.

Mentees Take Note!

Remember, you are reading this book not to place eternal blame onto your toxic mother. Neither are you trying to heal by accessing the best mentoring available. Your healing is a disciplined journey to love others boldly—and that includes your mentor. As you consider asking someone to mentor you, keep in mind that you must be the best mentee you can. His time and life are just as important as yours. Your job is to settle into a mentor/mentee relationship where you can continue to grow in virtue and integrity, benefiting from being loved boldly as much as you develop your ability to love. Believe it or not, the U.S. government has a site that compiles seven lists of character-istics of a good mentee.[41] The third list includes, but is not limited to, these characteristics and advice:

1. Be prepared for your mentoring sessions.
2. Establish a mutually agreeable plan for mentoring sessions, including how much time each of you need if a session has to be postponed.
3. Let your mentor know who you are.
4. Focus on the relationship, rather than outcomes.
5. Ask direct questions about what you most want to know.
6. Practice learning from anyone.

7. Listen with an open mind.

8. Ask curious questions.

9. Take notes.

10. Provide context and brief updates to help your mentor to understand you.

11. Respect your mentor's boundaries.

12. Follow up on agreements.

13. Say "thank you!"

One of the lists suggests mentees "pass it along." So, what does it look like to be a good mentor to others.

Mentoring Younger Men

For the purposes of this book, let's stick to our need to mentor younger men regarding how they are healing from toxic mothers. It is for all intents and purposes an obligation. We sons are reading this book because we have had spotty support for the healing process. If we start mentoring younger men, they will develop healthy RTLB and practice those into their marriages and parenting and places of employment. There are many mentor certification programs that appear in a simple Google search. The majority of them are related to business or youth, but relatively few specify help for specific issues except for the obvious and more public ones such as substance abuse and gang prevention. The prevalence of programs, however, verifies that there are universals in good mentoring. For example, the Franchise Growth Partners[42] website lists 10 qualities of a good mentor.

1. Willingness to share skills, knowledge, and expertise.

2. Demonstrates a positive attitude and acts as a positive role model.

3. Takes a personal interest in the mentoring relationship.

4. Exhibits enthusiasm in the field.

5. Values ongoing learning and growth in the field.

6. Provides guidance and constructive feedback.

7. Respected by colleagues and employees in all levels of the organization.

8. Sets and meets ongoing personal and professional goals.

9. Values the opinions and initiatives of others.

10. Motivates others by setting a good example.

If you are in any field, find a younger man to mentor. It is the best gift you can give to a young man and it will challenge you to keep growing and healing yourself, whether your mentee is a young sales associate or a man in need of serious healing work. My mentor, Ralph, was a banker, and many of his mentees needed help navigating their professional world, but all of us carried very different kinds of baggage. Another advantage of mentoring younger men is that you will begin to see that toxic mothers aren't the only problem, and many times they are not the worst. Being a young man's mentor might help him find a path to healing completely separate from being their mother's collateral damage. Live your life with integrity and focus on the issues that you can control, and your life will bring you in the path of young men to mentor.

Dom: One of My Mentees

I mentor several young men. I met Dom when he was fresh out of college. His bicultural background intrigued me, but I quickly forgot about him. He was simply the friend of my friends' twins. When I received a friend request from Dom on Facebook, I clicked accept with little thought since he was in his mid-twenties by then. Then, I started seeing posts that warped me into my adolescence when my sister's bipolar disorder dismantled our family. Bold love, remember? I messaged Dom directly for two reasons. First, he had begun to announce publicly that he, indeed, was struggling with bipolar disorder. Second, he was moving to South Carolina simply to be in the ministry with his engaged friend. No job, no goals, nothing but to be the friend like Jonathan was with King David—sacrificial, holding David accountable for reigning with integrity. I told Dom my history and was honest in saying his move felt a bit manic. I wanted to make sure he was making the decision wisely, since it seemed he was setting himself up to be a third wheel with his friend and the friend's fiancée. I simply offered to be a sounding board if he so needed. He wrote back and we talked for hours on the phone, agreeing that he could call me to be a reality check of his thinking while he sought balance for his mental health. This is my follow-up to him afterward:

> I vowed from a bad experience never to give advice unless I was asked. You asked so I delivered. I am flattered you even indulged me. I am confident that God will complete the work He has begun in you whether you go to SC or not. I'd love to know how to pray. Thanks for the details of your life. Forgive me if I've overstepped my bounds and begun sounding like a father, but you leave a LOT for a man to be proud of, Dom. Beneath the shadow of HIS wings you can rejoice. Based on your life circumstances right now, I'm glad to be reminded of the same. August 23, 2011.

Now, ten years later, I've walked with him through breakups, marriage, buying a home, and now currently, starting a business and more. It has been a privilege to see him embrace his illness and live his life well.

Ben: Another Mentee

Ben's mother was our infertility nurse. For those of you who have experienced infertility, your nurse becomes your blood relative, best friend, health care provider and counselor altogether. So, naturally, her thirteen-year-old Ben went trick-or-treating with our family. He was pudgy and shy, and I just thought he was being adolescent. But his mother quickly revealed that he was failing school and was going down the wrong paths. So, I suggested to her that I could teach Ben some study habits, tutor him and see what happened. Ben's resistance led us to switch directions. When he was fifteen, I leveled with him and he opened himself up to change and healing. I told him he can talk to me about anything, and I would keep it safe unless he was going to hurt himself or someone else, he did something illegal or someone hurt him. I gave him a simple on-line career selection assessment based on things like interests, grades, level of education, and more. When all was said and done, if Ben were to continue along his current path, he would be qualified to train for a videographer position at a public television station. He turned his life around and started doing better in high school. We continue meeting to this day but not as regularly since he has been to chef school, baking school, worked at world-renown restaurants, and more. Now, at thirty years old, he enlightens me with his philosophy and faith and we have a hilarious time together. He even went back to writing poetry and music.

Neither of these mentees came looking for me. And, I found my own mentor by seeking help from a therapist. The important thing here is that we who are on the path of healing from our toxic mothers ought to have our radars on to locate a struggling son.

If you connect with a mentor, don't squander your fortune by keeping it for yourself. Ralph inspired me to be a mentor, and I believe it has made a difference in the lives of young sons. As you move on, help someone younger move on as well!

How Do I Know It Is Working? Mentoring Alejandro

By the time Alejandro, a very bright African American young man, showed up on my doorstep needing a place to stay for a few weeks, I had taken the bite out of my bitterness and shame. I had truly embraced how examining my own heart while being honest about whether I was loving AND being loved boldly is the only way to know I am still on the right path. We had an empty guest house, so I told Alejandro yes. He moved in with very little and we hung out together over dinner or neighborhood visits quite often.

But it took only days for me to learn two things. First, he had a strained relationship with his mother, anger toward his divorced parents, resentment toward his brother, and he clung readily to a victimhood that made it difficult to know how he was really doing. Second, his politics aligned on the total other end of the spectrum as mine.

With those dynamics came many assumptions he had about me. A conservative certainly cannot love someone like him. My racism is so deeply rooted that I'll never understand social justice. And so on. When I asked him about his social justice agenda, he condemned people that looked like me right to my face, as if he did not acknowledge that I was attempting to love him unconditionally no matter what. It hurt, but I knew I had matured, because his hurtful comments only encouraged me to create better ways to restore him to health.

I did not shy from loving him boldly, attempting to get at the root of his estrangements, wanting to restore him to a better relationship at least with himself. He believed in God, he was friendly, yet super guarded.

After four weeks, it was clear he needed a more permanent residence, so we sat down and negotiated. He could stay in the house as long as he needed as long as he was working toward making his future more independent, and Marie and I deserved to know that simply because we did not want to squander our guest house on a free-loader. I offered to help him in any capacity as long as he was straight with me. I did not want a hustle nor did I want to enable, which is exactly what I told him.

Alejandro was excelling in a job that was not necessarily his passion, but he worked hard and earnestly. He really wanted to go to graduate school. So, I recommended he begin applying to the best and I would help him write the essays. Marie and I supported him financially through his master's and his PhD, but I realized that my ability to love others had matured during our time together. I had intentionally approached Alejandro to restore him to a better relationship with himself, with me, with others, and with God.

Alejandro Looks in the Mirror

One evening I dropped Alejandro off across town, but he lingered in the car because he wanted to tell me something. After hemming and hawing about how he didn't want to disappoint me, I told him he could not do that even if he tried. I loved him like a son and he has made me proud. He said, "But . . . I'm gay, and I'm sure you don't want to be associated with that." I said, "And?" We discussed that my job was to love him and not judge him and that he needed to reconcile with himself the shame he felt in front of people like me, especially when he made so many assumptions about people like me. He was restored to a better relationship with himself by experiencing an unconditional love that set him free.

Alejandro Reaches Out

With the maturity I was learning through my own healing, especially in the area of parenting, I did not need my ego stroked by the people I was choosing to love. But, Alejandro began to reach out to me, asking me for advice, consoling me during very sad times, and even inviting me to his PhD graduation. It very much reminds me of my relationship with Ralph, my mentor of so many years.

Alejandro Creates a Family

As Alejandro completed his formal education, I was able to help him navigate the many instances when he was being exploited or mistreated. I spoke bluntly to him about how he cowers to power-hungry people and gives himself and his ideas away, ideas that could generate revenue and publicity for him in his field. After helping him see the pattern, I told him, why don't you just create your own enterprise, and he did. Marie and I helped him only a little bit financially as he found people to work with him and for him and not against him. They became his family away from home. I am so grateful when he tells me how his colleagues and his friends now support him. He has not reconciled with his family at home, but, like this book suggests, there came a point when he had to let go of the dream of a healthy relationship with his mother, the one pushing most of the buttons.

Alejandro Walks with God

While Alejandro grew up in the church, he developed a mean, judgmental view of God, always disappointed in him. Currently, he has reconciled his sexual identity and his passion for social justice under the loving arm of a God Who loves him unconditionally. It started with the conversation in the car, but I never ceased to remind him that through faith, God does not see us as damaged goods but rather as His own children, heirs to the King of the Universe. He can stand tall and live his life proudly, and he can call me when he doubts himself. And he does.

I will always need a mentor in my own life, but, if I concentrate on loving others well, I can and should mentor others whose lives have been negatively influenced by a toxic mother.

CHAPTER 11

SEEK WELL AND CELEBRATE WHAT YOU FIND

With newly formed RTLB, you are in control of what you seek and find. When we are seeking, we have something specific we are trying to find. As you walk into your healing journey, seek intentional things intentionally. With purpose! Your life may seem fragmented, but if you are working consistently and progressively on your RTLB, you can exercise the freedom to seek what you've learned you need and you will set yourself up to find healing overall. And you will also encounter great things such as wisdom, integrity, loving relationships, peace, and so much more. You will know you are moving on when you unknowingly or naturally turn to seek something else that brings you joy or that loves someone boldly.

This cycle keeps you from stagnating. I'm not speaking for all men, but I fall prey to the thinking that "I've arrived." You may have heard how men tend to want to find a solution instead of listening to and loving the one stating the problem or struggle. What you seek is not a solution but a confidence that you are developing healthy habits and lifestyle choices that free you up to exercise a newly formed energy to become the man you conceive. As you recognize you are beginning to find those things you have sought, welcome them with open and unabashed arms. *And celebrate when you realize you have found something more.*

Seek Adventure

When you seek adventure, two things occur. First, you inevitably meet new people with whom you can share yourself while you practice loving boldly. An adventure takes you out of your comfort zone where you must learn new things. Not only do you learn new knowledge and skills like rock climbing or hiking or playing an instrument, but befriending the new people you encounter will always challenge your RTLB in ways you've never considered. Second, seeking adventure forces you to see that your "solutions" to love others and develop integrity need adapting for every new situation. It keeps you from acquiring the mindset that you ARE healed instead of enjoying the journey of personally healing.

The Coin Club

After my father died, my mother gave me his coin collection. I decided to finish some of his series in his honor. After I did that, I became more interested in coin collecting. So, I jumped into two "adventures" that, for me, were monumental. I called an acquaintance to ask if he would accompany me to my first meeting of a coin collecting club in our city. And, then we went. I was out of my element and still am. But, when I go, I am reminded that I can befriend these salty people in a new environment as much as I can anyone with the help of God's Grace and my new RTLB. By stepping out, I developed a stronger friendship with my acquaintance and I began to look forward to hearing the coin club members' stories; it made me miss my dad in such a sweet way. Lately, I've been sad that COVID-19 has shut the club down for over a year. The fact that I was growing to love others and walk into an unfamiliar context willingly was not just evidence that I was healed. *It was a celebration that I was moving on.*

Sometimes Weaknesses Invite Healing Strength

During the last six months with my mother, I discovered that she loved parties, she loved making new friends, and that she had felt limited while she was with my father. She was always taking her fiancée on adventures and social outings. She also was feeding me the confusing demands that no one was to know she was sick, she did not want me to give her a memorial service when she was gone, and she made me swear I would comply.

I said OK but wanted to see if "seeking a new adventure" would help heal me and her some simultaneously. So, I suggested she give herself a party. I sucked at planning parties, but I needed to grow in that area. She immediately refused, but a month later, she agreed only if I helped her have a "friends and family" party and not the goodbye party I was envisioning. I conceded. I told her I would pay for everything and help her as much as I could to plan, but she would have to ask for the help she needed, otherwise I was not going to butt in. On one of my visits, we took my printed invitations that she approved and we hand delivered them in her neighborhood. The adventure? I let her drive the golf cart! Blind, yes! Frail at eighty-five pounds, yes! She had an out-of-town friend help her write all the addresses the week before and we went door to door delivering them. We even knocked on a lady's door and found out she doesn't even know my mother. Mom invited her anyway. She had forgotten to charge the golf cart, so I pushed while she steered to finish the deliveries. We interviewed and hired the quirkiest DJ I've ever met. I was out of my element, but it was helping me facilitate both of us seeking adventure and celebrating what we've discovered instead of dwelling on our toxic past.

The whole process gave her a purpose and it gave me a context to let my RTLB feel natural and not contrived. She had a blast, and we spoke of it regularly for two months until she became unresponsive only days before she died. I helped restore her to a better version of herself where she celebrated people instead of condemned them. I helped unite her living siblings in the God-forsaken state of Arizona. I helped her have peace that she could depend on God and me to carry her to a time when she can't sit up in bed and she's ready to meet Jesus. She was happy. It felt like healing. We were both moving on.

Seek Wisdom

How will you know if you have found anything when you seek wisdom? I have many people who throw knowledge my way, but I would never consider it "wisdom." When I need insight, information, advice, validation, or whatever, I want it to come from people and sources I respect. I want to see the "wisdom" at work in their life. I want to hear what they've found as a result of seeking the wisdom they are now sharing. I also want to be conscious of my acceptance or denial of the wisdom being offered.

My mother constantly offered me the "wisdom" that "rich people don't make good friends." I found out during my mother's last days that she "censored" my friendship with an amazing high school buddy: Barry Goldman. In comparison, Barry was rich, but he practiced the art of friendship so well with people from all walks of life. I constantly feared he would discover my mother's infinite "wisdom" and turn away from our friendship. I kept this secret hidden from him until this very moment. My mother was judging someone because of their social status. At fifty-five years old, I grieved tremendously when she told me that she would not let me go out as a teenager when she knew it was with a Goldman (I happened to like his sister too). The entire Goldman family loved me boldly, for which I am immensely grateful.

At thirty years old, after meeting with my mentor, Ralph, for over a year, he finally broke his vow of silence and gave me some "wisdom." He simply said, "Guy, you spend your life in misery trying to make up for the crap your parents put you through. Stop! You don't owe them anything. You can be the man you want to be with or without their approval. And, here's the kicker! Whether they approve of what you are doing or not, ***the best gift you can give your parents is to live your own life well.***" When those words of wisdom left Ralph's mouth they entered my ears after hearing his stories of longing for his father's approval, working hard to please his mother. He struggled with college choice, profession choice, wife choice, how to parent, how to handle his anger and confusion, and much more. Just Like Me! But he had also followed his own advice and became the best "dad" to orphans like me, and he had worked hard to be able to do exactly what he wanted to live his life well according to his RTLB and how God had designed him. That was the moment I learned to move on.

Seek Humility[43]

If you think you won't find anything of value when you seek humility, then you are not humble. You do not deserve royal treatment or reparations because of your toxic mother. When you feel the need to assert yourself, keep your pride in check. Nothing your toxic mother did to you or for you can take away the progress you make, but acting like the progress you make can bring you to impose your toxic RTLB on your mother is evidence you have gone too far. Remember the litmus test: love boldly! Does puffing yourself up help to restore your mother to any better relationship with anyone? She's toxic, remember? She's wired to respond vehemently when someone confronts her. You do not deserve humiliation, but you must find the line of humility and cross into it. You are too valuable to others and to God. They will always be there for you even if your mother attempts to crush you. Humility can be the impetus for walking away from humiliation. Learn the difference between them both and take responsibility when you find yourself in the pride zone. Moving arrogantly toward your toxic mother is a formula for disaster for you both. Moving on or away from your mother is best initiated with humility.

Seek Help

I reiterate this idea because it is of utmost importance. There are many sources (some of which are annotated in the last chapter) to help with healing emotions, wounds, mindsets, relationships, or whatever you are discovering needs healing. The issue is not necessarily knowing where to turn for such help, but rather knowing when.[44] My rule of thumb is, if you are asking honestly if now is the time, then now is the time!

After several periods of intensive therapy, I realized a pattern. A certain life crisis would come into my life, I would despair and then seek counseling. I would work very hard until that crisis dwindled a bit. Then, I paused the counseling until the next crisis. I learned from this pattern to seek a good counselor who would serve as a bridge during these up and down times. At our first visit, I handed him a very long list of every issue I think I had. I'm sure he knows of more, but he's waiting for me to bring them up. I had gone to him for a specific reason (of course, looking for a solution, not a healing tool). We met, I worked hard, he encouraged me to experiment with my new healing in the real world until the next time I needed him. Just knowing he's out there helps me sort out whether I'm still moving on from my toxic mother, but it also lets me explore my current life issues as well.

Individual counseling isn't the only help you can seek. Group therapy is great too.[45] When I was thirteen, my brother fifteen, and my sister seventeen, we ended up in family therapy. My sister had twice attempted suicide, almost overdosed several times, had had a mental breakdown reacting to an abortion that was still being kept a secret to my brother and me, and much more. I remember sitting in a circle with a counselor and a resident. They both would ask us questions, and we were allowed to say whatever we wanted. I was hypnotized by the idea that I could speak the truth and not be punished by my mother. My brother and I had already given each other the look of amazement that my mother was stripped of being able to spin or silence what we said. He and I left nothing on the table. My mother raged at us the whole week between sessions. After our third session, my mother told the therapist in front of us that we weren't coming back. I cried—because it felt so freeing to simply tell the truth about what was on my heart. That is the healing power of therapy.

Besides counseling, you can read books by select authors. There are so many out there on toxic parents and toxic parenting. Many do not address you directly as a son with unique needs and circumstances, but it is easy to apply the information in positive ways. Find people you trust to help you reflect on what input you might use to move the healing process on. Friends, mentors, clergy can help you heal too. Ultimately, you are responsible for your own healing, but you have spent a lifetime in the disease of your mother's toxicity. As above, be humble and wise about your need for outside help in moving on.

Seek Insight

Part of seeking help is seeking insight. This is not limited to insights of a personal nature. Focusing exclusively and completely on your own perspective leads to isolation and insulation. In your counseling you can explore insights you've gained about yourself during your own healing journey. Successes and failures provide you rich moments to seek insight into your RTLB, your relational style, your issues, and more. The key is to be honest and document those heightened moments. Many counselors are practicing Cognitive Behavioral Therapy (CBT) that helps you capture your motivations and emotions during intense exchanges and issues you have during your normal life tasks.[46] My CBT sessions with my counselor were greatly enriched by the fact that I took great discipline to journal explosive exchanges with my family and other people I was choosing to learn to love boldly. Then, with CBT, you can begin to experiment with different reactions in similar situations to see if you can accomplish your goals of mental and emotional health. It works.

But seek insight into your mother's toxic behavior too. This book provides one exercise to do that. Start a conversation with her if that's possible. Verify some of her "stories" with other relatives. Ask trusted friends who have seen you act and react to your mother's infringements. The general rule about seeking insight is that you not rely solely on your "personal, inward" insights. Seek with diligence, wisdom, and humility the observations and insights of those you've vetted through your RTLB. An outside view may reveal ways for you to love boldly at times and places you would not have considered beforehand.

Before my mother's illness, my healing journey brought me to a point where I could ask my mother the simple question: why? Why had she lied about my sister's abortion? Why does she despise rich people? Why does she mistrust everyone but attempt to keep them under control by catering to them? Over the course of a month, I encouraged my mother to visit me on her own to see if I could gain insight into my mother's craziness.

Inviting the Wolf?

In my father's presence, she constantly complained about his sickly condition and the fact that she could not do the things she wanted to do because she had to "stay behind and take care of [my] father." I finally had enough of her shaming him publicly in front of me! So, to the both of them, I said, "Dad, do you need Mom to be here for you if she comes to visit me?" He replied, "No, I can take care of myself." There! The truth was out, and it didn't match my crazy mother's delusions and guilt-mongering.

By exposing the truth that my dad didn't need my mother to babysit him while she did something she wanted to do (a grown-up approach to most human interactions), I was loving my father boldly. I gave him the platform to speak up for himself and against the oppression and shame coming from my toxic mother. He was restored to a better relationship with himself by my removing some of the shame and guilt my mother dumped on him so readily. I restored him to a better relationship with me by letting him know I was on his side, the side of truth and maturity and responsibility for our own decisions, actions, and attitudes.

So, Mom came for a week, just herself. We walked every day. In response to my questions, she consistently spoke about how she was still traumatized by her father. She recounted the same stories I had heard, the stories that moralized how she is doing so much better than she had it with her father. He was an alcoholic. He was mentally ill. He verbally, emotionally, and physically abused each and every one of his children until they left home at very young ages. She was the fourth of six children. When her two youngest siblings started to become the targets of their father's abuse, she protected them by letting him abuse her instead. I had heard those stories forever. She would always conclude them with, "But, Guy, he had a genius IQ." I never understood what that meant, and never will now.

With some personal insight into myself, and with the framework of my mother's tragic life, I wanted to love her well. I simply laid out the question gently, lovingly, and boldly. I wanted to help her connect with herself, gain insight into her own psyche and perhaps restore her to possess a less toxic commitment to control me and everyone—our actions and our impressions of her and her character. I was hoping she could see some of the toxic RTLB she had adopted while being victimized in her youth.

"Mom, your dad was a monster. These stories are grotesque. No one should have to go through what you did with him. You survived.

You have grown kids. They're relatively functional. You own your house. You have great friends. But, I have to ask you this question. Where was your <u>mother</u> while your father was abusing you? Why don't you ever talk about her? Why do I hear immense blame only on your father for your emotional struggles? I need to be frank with you. I almost blame your mother more for being so negligent, sitting back and watching while your father unleashed evil upon evil."

She wept. Her first words? "Guy, I never wanted to be that for my own children. I never wanted to stand by and let you guys get hurt, let you guys be abused! I wanted to give you the love and attention I never got so I could prove to my father that he was pathetic! That's why I married your father. He needed me so much. He was immature, he needed attention, and he was never abusive to me. He was calm and controlled. I had a hard time trusting everyone, but he wanted to give me what I wanted: stability and kids."

"So, do you spend a lot of time trying to undo what was done to you? Do you try to help us kids avoid the pain you suffered?

"I guess."

"Well, I would think it's easier to focus on the physical abuse of your father more than it is the silent neglect from your mother. Have you thought about how that has affected you? I'm not saying she didn't love you, but have you thought about what kind of life you decided to have because your mother was not there for you? I'm sure it was a lot of pressure to stay involved in our lives and protect us from your childhood demons when Dad wasn't that engaged, Lisa had so many problems, Mark and I rebelled and drifted away feeling neglected, and you are left feeling the blame. I'm sorry if you feel I've blamed you for being negligent. I forgive you if you feel you have been. I understand you've done the best you can, and I love my life, past, present, and future. Whatever happened to you while you were a child was not your fault. Whatever happened to me as a child was not my fault. But, how we react to our childhood *is* our responsibility. You decided you would undo the abuses and give us the best life ever. I decided I had to do everything on my own because you and dad were consumed with Lisa's mental and physical illnesses. My reaction to how you raised me is not your fault. I've got to find ways to love you in spite of my angry heart. I need your forgiveness. But,

I need to live my own life in a way that helps me move on from all this blame and guilt and shame and sadness. I just need you to know that I'm trying."

By having that very conversation, I gained some insight and I shared some insight. I would not have found that insight had I not sought it with intention. Seek insight!

Seek Restoration (Bold Love)

It's no surprise that my mother was the last one in my family of origin with whom I reconciled completely. Upon each of their deaths, I have realized the power of restoring and being restored. I caught the vision of Bold Love (thank you, Dan Allender) way before my sister died and went to work redesigning my RTLB with everything I learned along the way.

Lisa

Lisa, bipolar, brain damaged from an accident, brain fried from illicit drugs, had no boundaries, but neither did she have any guile. So, when I decided to love her boldly it was as simple as exploring the truth with her. I could say things just as outlandish as she, and we quickly respected the transparency with which we could relate.

When she would call me to ask if she and her children could live with me, I would ask first if she was taking her meds or if she was in a manic state. Then, I would reiterate my deep aversion to two families living in the same household, especially *her* family. I was simply too tired and had too much baggage for her to live that close to me. She accepted my view gracefully, and I was able to apply my own RTLB, mainly, those of being generous and protecting myself and my own family from the dysfunction and chaos and collateral damage that always followed my sister's presence. I spoke strategically and gleefully with her about what she needed, and could usually provide material things. I told my parents that Marie and I would be glad to be her "guardian" when they were dead and gone. And, with my sister, I could ask for and offer insight into our toxic mother. Although she was not conscious when I told her goodbye, I regret nothing of my relationship with Lisa, but it was difficult to move on. I grieved appropriately and justifiably, especially since she was at her prime of healing herself. I miss her dearly.

Dad

Before my father's quintuple bypass surgery, the doctors told my mother and me that my father was to eat or drink absolutely nothing. They specified, not liquids, not ice, not gum, not even Chapstick. The very second after the doctors left the room, my mother went to my father's bedside and spooned piles of ice into his mouth. She slapped me when I told her to stop. From that point on, my goal to love my father boldly had two concerns in mind. First, I needed to protect him from my mother. Her behavior was turning into a black widow's. Second, I needed to find ways to love him boldly in his defeated state: oppressed and manipulated by my mother, sickly and morbidly overweight, sedentary and socially isolated and protected by my mother.

My conversations with him were frank with a focus on listening to and encouraging him. It worked. He called me without my mother prompting or controlling. I would send him coins and I paid for him to have a personal trainer at a nearby gym. As my own healing progressed, I could talk to him about my misgivings with the way my mother treated him. He responded honestly owning his resignation and passivity and even his remorse over having been unfaithful. He knew she was not going to change, but he was committed to being faithful until the end. I respected that.

Then, years later in the hospital for the fourth time in twelve days, he called me to his bedside and completed our restoration. He loved me boldly by asking me if he needed to ask for my forgiveness for anything he might have done against me. He assured me that he loved the man I had become. He told me he wanted to die the next time he went septic and he needed my help. He believed that even though my mother had been reckless with his rehab from the heart issues, he suspected she was going to keep him alive on life support even though he had signed a DNR. I assured him I would make sure she honored it.

I knew then the gift he had given me. He restored me to a healthier man, confident in the quality of the work I had done to love and honor my parents. I thanked him for being my father, for loving me and for helping me with this sad prospect of saying goodbye to him forever, for the last time. With his humble and brave act to speak bold love into our relationship, I was able to move on with no regrets. I miss him dearly.

Mom

My quest to love my mother boldly paid off. During the last two weeks of her being coherent, she asked me to dial her friends and family to say goodbye to them for the last time. I asked her what I could do to help her "let go." Katy, our wonderful hospice nurse, had told us that Mom would grow calmer as she let go of "things." So, Mom and I talked about the things she was holding onto. She didn't want me to change her diaper. We asked her friend to be there if I needed. She wanted me to draft a letter to Mark to tell him to get substance abuse counseling before she gave him his third of her leftover bank account. Even in her frail state, my bold love directed me to warn against it. I told her that God's Grace to us has no conditions, and, if she was wanting to leave a legacy, it should be about Grace and not about attaching strings to a love he probably already resented. She agreed. We spent the last two weeks singing hymns from the TV gospel station karaoke style. Back and forth, we loved each other boldly. This book is evidence that I've moved on. I miss her dearly.

Mark

Thirty-one days after my mother's death, my brother died of a hidden, latent aneurysm in his brain stem. My relationship with him was divided between Drunk Mark and Sober Mark. My commitment to Bold Love challenged me to love both. Mark and I were bonded by our disdain for our toxic mother. In his strange, alcohol-confused way, he loved me well, always caring for my well-being. When we were neglected teenagers, he told people at school not to mess with me. In his crazy brain, he believed he was protecting me from those bullies out there who thought I was a sissy, probably because I was not athletic, I was quite verbally intelligent, and . . . I was a sissy.

The minute my mom died, I called to tell him. His first question to me was, "So, how are you?" I answered by telling him the details of how Mom passed, and he said in his loving, brotherly way, "Noooo . . . How are YOU? You told me what happened. I want to know how YOU'RE doing?" I cried. I realized at that moment he was loving me boldly. I responded, "I'm OK . . . exhausted and sort of glad it's over." And, in a very "therapist" way, he said, "So, you're relieved. Right?"

"Yes, I'm relieved. It's been hell, and I don't think my body or my soul could have taken much more."

"OK, so you're relieved. You know what I am? . . . FREE! And I'm looking forward to not having her in my life anymore!"

I was sad, but I totally understood. So, I continued down the path to love him boldly. "I'm looking forward to hanging out with you when we don't have to talk about HAZEL WORLD! Let's plan a fishing trip, you and I and your boys!" He agreed. Those were the last words I spoke to him. It's been hard to move on because I keep thinking of "what-if" questions. Both of us were most affected by my mother's escapade, and neither of us were able to move on for very long together as brothers, to see where it might have taken us. God is in control, and is healing my grief and regrets, but I will miss him with all my heart. He was the last link to my family of origin and the last hope to see good come out of evil. Love Boldly! You never know how much time you have to find joy in restoring yourself and others to a better relationship with God.

Find Your Own Life

This is a composite way to say, "Find your purpose, mission, meaning, and calling." What is your purpose in life?[47] What mission or missions does that purpose present to you? How does what you do for a profession or job fit into your purpose and mission? Do you believe you were designed or destined for one mission? Where does that calling come from? Does your professional status fit into your new life plan and rules-to-live-by? Are you taking advantage of everything you can to determine your own unique set of strengths and personality traits? Does your job allow you to continue the job of healing and transforming yourself, of examining your life with the help of other sources? Remember, find your calling, not hers. As you move closer to executing your calling, you also move closer to the joy of fulfilling that calling. And, as you move further and further away from her limitations, you move further away from the environments and RTLB that limit your healing. If you are seeking things like this, you will find your own life. Leave the life of victimhood and move on to become your own hero.

Find Joy

Find joy! Expect it! Not happiness. Happiness passes with the next moment. If you are seeking to love boldly and be loved boldly, you will find joy. There is joy in knowing you are being restored while restoring others. There is even more joy in knowing God does the restoring, not us. We are called to love Him and enjoy Him forever. And, that is best done and most tangibly seen when we build others up, healing while healing others. There is joy in seeking adventure. The insight you gain from having to trust in something bigger than your small vat of experience provides you comfort and joy. You are a survivor, and you are wiser because of it. The wisdom you seek will show you the joy of moving on and not holding on to the past.

Find Respect

When you love boldly, you find respect from others. They will respect how you have taken on a higher calling, not only to heal from your toxic mother, but to transform yourself into a wise, humble, loving human being. When you seek the help from professionals because you have looked honestly at your life and admit your need to love better or to create better RTLB, the professionals respect you and others are inspired to do the same kind of search for insight. Over time, your healing journey will lead you to respect yourself more and more while loving others more and more boldly, including your toxic mother. Your mother may not respect you along the way, but your healthy respect for yourself and others will show her you have moved on with your life.

Find Your People

Finally, seeking the right things, some of which are listed above, will ultimately result in you finding "your people" and your God. Remember my friend whose toxic mother demanded she and her sisters comply with her demand for a DFH (Dysfunctional Family Holiday) as my friend calls it? My friend, "Jane," has found her people. Her people do not look or think the same, and she nurtures her relationships with ALL of us. She knows the importance of having found her people, and as she loves each of us boldly, she tests and refines all her RTLB with Grace, truth, and humility. Her family dynamics have left such a sad impression on her life that she considers "her people" to be her family. If you do not feel as though your efforts are helping you find your support team or "your people," seek insight again. Get help again. Humble yourself again. Revise your RTLB again. Don't despair. Move on with the hope and confidence that you are a work in progress as long as you are working on healing.

CHAPTER 12

KNOCK AND WAIT FOR IT TO BE OPENED

It's the waiting that's hard. But so is the search for ideas and activities worthy of knocking. Knocking on what? Knocking why? In healing, you must have the courage to take risks, especially if you are engaging your toxic mother at all. Whether it is your mother or a new friend or a new love interest, you can love boldly and adventurously using your RTLB. Keep in mind that your initiative . . . your "knocking" . . . simply reflects you and your RTLB, and your "waiting" simply provides Grace, truth, time, and patience for both you and the other to react. When you reach out and knock, know that it is in giving that you receive. Relationships develop and blossom over time. Knocking once and expecting anything in return, especially in this crazy social media-driven society, is not realistic. Even in the Bible verse from which this chapter title is adapted, the original verb in the Greek was in the progressive: "Keep knocking!" Knock in random and different ways. Knock in original or personal ways. Just knock.

It is not selfish to think about WHAT you are waiting for when you knock. If you are knocking on someone's door and expecting fun, enjoyable hobby time and the other wants hot, steamy romance, then you must reevaluate if and how you might knock again. Usually, knocking translates into a version of loving boldly. For example, when I sense a young man needs insight and safety to design his own set of RTLB, I offer to meet with him for lunch. After knocking, I make it a point to tell him up front one of the reasons I invited him was to discuss my observations and my willingness to help in any way I can. Then, I let it go. Many men over the years have taken me up on my offer, many have not. But I keep in mind that their life is their life. They call the shots.

Some men go in and out of my life as they meet new crises in their lives—very similarly to how I treated my relationship with my mentor, Ralph. I remain faithful to my promise. I take a risk when I offer, as sometimes the offer is simply too much for the man to grasp, either in denial or in shame; he just can't accept. It is sometimes the first and last time I interact meaningfully with that man. It is something I've considered before knocking. I never back down when I suspect someone is hurt, depressed, or suicidal. I knock. If we don't knock, then we are waiting for nothing to happen, and nothing is sure to happen. Here are a few ideas of knocking and suggestions for what you might anticipate.

1. Send a creative gift for no reason and expect no reply.

My mother constantly reminded me that my "rich" lifestyle made me judge them. She blamed my "snobbery" for never visiting. When I would talk about a Broadway play I attended with my immediate family, she would always sarcastically say, "Well, we have Sight and Sound. It's the best reproductions of Bible stories on the stage. We go to them with our friends all the time." You can imagine it was not a "share a similar story" statement but rather a screw you and your Broadway culture, we have our own culture and we're fine with it." Marie and I heard there was a production of the Passion of Christ in Lancaster, so we bought six tickets, invited two friends of theirs, and surprised them with a dinner theater performance. We left the next day. No comments about how "dinner theater" was beneath us or "you guys probably don't think Sight and Sound comes close to Broadway." Marie and I vowed not to entertain that discussion. We simply enjoyed the performance, my parents, and their friends.

On another occasion, my son and I were headed to Hershey, Pennsylvania, because he needed to do "research" on his school project's famous American, Milton Hershey. I took him to the Hershey chocolate museum so he could prepare his second-grade speech in the first person. I called my parents and told them we were coming and asked if they'd like to join us on the tour, just to see Matthew. Remember, my mother had put him in danger, she had bitched at me for keeping my children away from her, and she constantly used my sister's mental illness to reject any knocking I would initiate.

So, creatively, I schemed. I called my sister and told her to encourage my parents to go and that she would like to join them to see us too. I reserved a room for them at the Hershey Hotel, along with a couple's chocolate body wrap and massage from the spa. They came to tour with us, and we ate brunch in the hotel. Then, Lisa brought in two suitcases she had packed for them and I surprised them with their weekend getaway. Mom took me aside and said, "You know we can't do this. We can't leave your sister alone." Remember, she also complained to me constantly that she never gets to spend time with my father alone because of my sister. I simply laid out the plan. You can stay here this whole weekend. I've lined up a nurse to check in on Lisa. She and her kids have a ride home, you have suitcases for the weekend. It's all up to you. Matthew and I have to get back to the airport."

If you know me, you'd know I'm quite creative except when it comes to making plans. I admit, I needed my wife to help me with logistics, but the creativity paid off. They stayed and said they enjoyed the time. I had succeeded in helping restore their relationship with each other just a bit.

2. Welcome safe people into your life and expect to form healthy, mutual friendships.

If you are sincere in your efforts to work toward healing, you will already be welcoming safe people into your life. As you do, define in your head and according to your RTLB what a healthy, mutual friendship would be with them. Define "healthy" and "mutual" for each relationship. Every person you welcome will be different, and you must treat each appropriately.

But, I must say that mostly every healthy relationship I've created in my healing journey has been mutual. The context of each relationship determines the nature of its health and reciprocity. For example, when I am coaching a teacher, I do not expect them to become my friend. When I am mentoring a kid, I want to make sure I am as vulnerable as can be without scaring him or revealing anything my wife would not approve of. I've concluded in my life that if I am loving another person boldly and being loved boldly by that same person, then somewhere in one of us, our messiness will bear its ugly teeth and relationships are being restored along the way. The closer you become to a person, the more potential you have to see and experience the yuck in their lives. The key here is the expectation that healthy, mutual relationships can and will form while you live and love. It will be up to you to nurture each one the way you see fit, including determining if the relationship itself is better avoided or terminated.

3. Rekindle a beloved or broken friendship and wait for healing to occur.

Rekindling a former friendship is both humbling and exciting when filtered through our Bold Love framework. Openness, integrity, humility, and restoration are beautifully challenged with this motive. I have a friend, Hunter, who seriously hurt me at a very vulnerable time in my life. His actions set my entire family on a terribly dark path for years. The details are not relevant here. I knew I was moving on in healing when he called me to see if we could meet. I knew it was to ask me for money (he worked in development), and I was prepared to accept the invitation to meet, but I was not giving him any money. He agreed, and I made us turkey salads at my house. After all these years apart, I was still waiting for healing to occur in my relationship with Hunter. I was vulnerable with him once, and it backfired badly. But, with healthy RTLB, I decided to love, forgive, and be very honest about everything we discussed. We agreed to meet again, and a month later, he was teaching me how to run a boat at the beach. I cherish his friendship more every day.

4. Join an interest or hobby group and expect to grow personally and connect easily with others.

Or, create an interest or hobby group of your own! When I first started out in voiceover, I needed a way to get better feedback than simple rejections from auditions. So, I created a group of voiceover artists that met in my home studio where we critiqued each other's former or current auditions. We learned voice acting techniques. That is the beauty of being a curriculum specialist. I can easily see what needs to be taught and how, but learning the content takes initiative, ingenuity, and creativity.

Even online! I wanted to learn the finer details of coin grading, so I joined a Facebook group that looked promising. I quickly learned two things about the people on the site. First, they talk in jargon and acronyms that mean nothing to me. Second, there are some really mean, crusty people who treat others almost as toxically as my mother did me. After scrolling for several weeks, I got up the nerve to ask a question to the facilitator of the group. I was embarrassed to ask what a simple abbreviation meant. He immediately responded with kindness, encouragement, and the information I needed. I went back to find his responses to others, and they consisted of him threatening to kick members out of the group if they continue to bully or demean other members. His replies were inspiring to everyone: integrity. And, it was easy to find many who were toxic.

After doing the work to heal thus far, I can more easily spot a toxic person and more readily welcome those I know to be safe and healthy. This is another byproduct of moving on. Remember, it will be easy to connect around mutual interests, but you must scrutinize with your RTLB whether the connection is appropriate.

5. Knock on the door of the animal shelter and wait to learn the healing of selfless love.

Watch this YouTube video: "After Given 5 Years to Live, an Overweight Man is Prescribed a New Diet: A Dog." It is surprisingly genuine. You see a man discuss what adopting a shelter dog can do for a person who has been socially isolated and downtrodden because of his weight. Doesn't that sound like a son's response to his toxic mother? Think about what the act of generating a new set of RTLB did for you. It opened the door for you to interact with others, test out the ways to be healthy, improve your ability to love boldly, help you be more receptive to being loved boldly, develop a respectful integrity, and more. By adopting a dog, the man in this video changed his relationship to food, socializing, exercise, habits, and so much more. The parallels are astounding. I quickly sensed the potential benefits of adopting a pet, but I'm allergic to dogs and cats. So, with my children, we've had a variety of other animals such as fish, lizards, rabbits, turtles, sugar gliders, sea monkeys, but not birds. For every pet we've hosted, my son, who is also allergic to dogs and cats, would always say, "But, Dad, lizards don't love you back."

He's right! It would heal even more to see your dog respond to your love by loving you unconditionally back. But, the act of caring for something as dependent as a pet puts you in a proper mindset to make sure you are taking care of yourself well so you can take good care of the pet. And, I've made great friendships by having my pets. I made sure our pets helped us to socialize with others no matter what. The lessons were invaluable.

6. Plan a vacation for you or her but create a respite greater than that.

Get yourself out of your element or help your mother get out of hers. You not only need time away from her, but you can spend that time in self-care of any sort. You might feel rested; you might not. Remember that a vacation is temporary, but respite is found in the inside. Use your healing RTLB to create a space, a routine, an experience, a meditation, or anything else that you can escape to when you are feeling unrested. Believe it or not, mine is word game apps. I know that sounds strange, but I've had to tell my wife specifically how and when I retreat to them, like when I'm stressed. It was off the charts while my mother was alive. I also write random letters of encouragement, sometimes by hand but always personal and specific. Another respite of mine is swimming. Still another is making a complete Thanksgiving dinner at any time of the year.

Whatever that place or experience is, claim it as a respite. It is yours and no one else's. Let your people know. Let your mother know if you think it would contribute to loving her boldly. I didn't. When she would catch me in my respite zone, I let her criticize me and my activity, but nothing can poison these places or experiences. Call it a safe space, a happy place, or whatever you want. Only you need to know that you can go there. And then go there. Learn the signs to know when.

When I was going to Arizona every other week, the stress would begin to accumulate before I would arrive. My mother would dote all over me but complain that she was losing her independence as she weakened. I would assure her that I was there to make her life easier and that she should save her energy for herself. I can take care of us.

It just wasn't happening. Instead, it was a dance that escalated in intensity until Mom would snap back into her Hazel World behaviors, and for the rest of the week, it was misery. I met one of my mother's dear friends who obviously understood some of the dynamics and she took me aside to ask if I needed help. I said immediately, "Yes!" She agreed to come to Mom's house for one and a half hours twice a day so I could swim, write, or sleep. Patty was a good and faithful friend to me *and* my mother. With her help, I could move on through the rest of the week having recharged physically, mentally, and/or emotionally. I didn't know that "time away from Mom" is a respite, but I quickly learned my need to plan it and how to redeem that time. There is nothing wrong with needing respite to continue fueling your moving on.

CHAPTER 13

CONCLUSION

Final Word from the Author

My mother was a complex person. She loved me strongly and deeply, but she feared the thought that I could have subsumed the generational toxicity she so naively attempted to mitigate. When I would bring up even the smallest piece of my dark and downtrodden heart or actions, she would interject that I was such a good baby. She outright denied the truth of my shady past. She claimed that with me, she "had finally learned to parent and love." She couldn't handle it when I spoke of my illicit drug use or sales. When my brother would corner me into admitting my own sexual escapades, she would be embarrassed for me and make the excuse that I was young.

When I took control of my own healing, I finally realized I didn't need to convince my mother of my dark side. Instead, I could just become the man I wanted to be, finding joy in loving and being loved boldly. Neither did I need to convince her that what she did to me was evil or unforgivable. My job was to love. I have forgiven my mother completely and can now recall with gratitude the beauty and blessings my mother bestowed onto me.

I have the fondest memories of her mothering me, and I make sure I do not taint them with my negative responses to her toxic side. One of my earliest memories is of me on the floor with a small plastic baggie, several Wonder Bread bags, and a pair of scissors. No, she wasn't negligent. I was precocious and safe with grade school materials, even at the age of four. She would show me how fun it was to cut out the colorful circles from the Wonder bags. I did it for hours and collected them in the small baggie. She showed me how to cut things out of the Sears catalog and fold the clips into tiny squares. She would fill the sink with water and let me drop each folded picture into the water and watch it unfold like magic. She noticed I taught myself to write cursive letters from the *Highlights* magazine. And, while babysitting four other children, she took the time to teach me to write the letters that I didn't know while at the same time encouraging me to continue reading at a very young age. She defended me when I was neglected or mistreated by teachers or bullies. She stayed up with me all night to help me start and finish a major project I had forgotten was due the next morning. I got an A.

My mother was also social and festive, celebrating anything and everything for those around her. This included Thanksgiving dinners for every kind of misfit imaginable: the abused, the poor, the immigrant (legal or not), the lonely, the newly divorced or widowed, and more. She welcomed everyone—a clear picture of Jesus Himself. She recruited the neighborhood children to perform plays under her deck "theater" stage. She directed the production and made the costumes. She made great friends wherever she went. She traveled with some, formed supper clubs with others, led civic club events, and even designed my high school graduation post-party casino with real-life gambling (and fake money, of course).

From her I learned to be creative and self-driven in my learning, never shying from a challenge. I am proud of her resourcefulness and have been inspired to reinvent myself several times during my midlife career crises. At the age of thirty-four, my mother passed the test to receive her driver's license for the first time. She used a broken typewriter to learn to type, she read books on how to write a résumé, she applied for a job as a receptionist at a trucking company, and immediately began moving up the ranks within that company and others. Ultimately, she became a coder for Pennsylvania Power and Light and retired with benefits enough to take her to Arizona and buy a seasonal park unit home while still living in her home in Pennsylvania. She showed me independence, resilience, and more.

In all this I hope it is clear that whether our mother is toxic or not, it is up to us to take ownership of how we have internalized her behaviors toward us. This book is not to help us blame our mothers for our miserable lives. *My life is not miserable.* I have directed my healing to ensure that. More and more consistently, I am choosing to love others boldly and appreciate the people I encounter while developing into a man of virtue and integrity. I have a long way to go, but I have all of eternity and an amazing God to help me enjoy being His child, loved wholly, boldly, and healed from the toxic effects of the whole world.

RESOURCES

This book is in no way thorough, but it does reframe a great deal of information that comes from sources of all kinds. Hopefully, while reading, you have encountered an idea or a reference that resonates with you and your circumstances with your toxic mother. Healing of this magnitude cannot be encased in a single, comprehensive volume, but the book introduces the healing principles by framing and consolidating them around the stories, processes, and information from many different resources and perspectives. Whether you are at the beginning of your journey to healing or have read this book to help you mentor someone who is, the following resources and references serve as a menu for anyone to plunge deeper into the healing journey. What follows are references for resources that can help you choose the next course of action with your healing process. First, there are different kinds of sources described and listed. Then, the footnotes from each chapter highlight sources related to the specific content to which they are attached.

Connect with the healing process in this book. Connect with the resources referenced in every chapter. You can own your own toxicity. You can redefine or create your own virtuous lifestyle rules-to-live-by. You can jump into the world equipped with those rules-to-live-by. That world is a playground where you can grow in virtue and integrity. You can enjoy freedom to love and live. You can welcome others into your life while you continue seeking healing input for your lifelong journey. And, you can discover the joy of loving and being loved boldly.

www.guyarcuri.com

Virtual Therapy:

Many psychology/therapy practices are offering therapy sessions through video conferencing platforms like Zoom. They are confidential and can be done at your convenience and in the comfort of your own home. This also helps you shop for the best fit therapist, not limited to a region or city. For example, you might do an internet search and locate a psychology practice with a terrific specialist who treats the issues you'd like to address. The counseling does not need to be addressed in person but can be done miles, states, or even countries apart. One such practice with many different kinds of specialists is Southeast Psych in Nashville or Charlotte: https://southeastpsychnashville.com and https://southeastpsych.com respectively.

There are many websites that compile multiple ones together and help you sort out the best one: https://www.betterhelp.com/helpme. Search wisely.

Assessing Your Need for a Therapist:

This site and more like it provide information for you to assess whether you should find outside help. Remember my rule of thumb: If you are asking, then you probably need help. But sites like this help you narrow your search to an appropriate kind of professional: https://www.mhanational.org/finding-help-when-get-it-and-where-go.

Self-Help Books and Websites

Obviously, I recommend self-help books to move you forward in your healing journey. I do, however, recommend you not pick them randomly nor read them by yourself. One of your overall goals is to learn to love others and be loved by others. You should, then, process the information of a self-help book with someone else: a friend, mentor, clergy, or therapist. As my mentor used to say, "Just because you have insight into the why of your feelings or behaviors doesn't mean you will use that information in a healthy manner." It is up to you to have the discipline and integrity to process self-help information, even that within this book, with the goal of practical and tangible application.

That said, you have several options after reading this self-help book.

1. Search Google or Amazon for a topic that you would like to process more deeply. Maybe it is a book or a speaker or a podcast. Ask a friend for help researching if you are not skilled in digital searches. My favorite is anything Rick Belden touches. I am indebted to his real and selfless contributions to sons of toxic mothers and anyone who loves them. Visit https://www.menandthemotherwound.com or rickbelden.com.

2. Ask your partner (pastor, clergy, friend, mentor, therapist) for a recommendation. Make sure you specify what your goal is. In fact, I recommend never reading a self-help book without setting a personal goal or objective for reading it.

3. Use the endnotes that follow to suggest related resources for your consumption. Go back to portions of this book that piqued your interest and then move to the endnotes related to the topics within the chapter. The endnotes follow the acknowledgments.

4. Visit my website: www.guyarcuri.com. There you can continue your healing in several ways. First, you can subscribe to the workbook for this book. Each exercise helps you apply one or more of the principles in this book as presented by the model in Figure 2. Completing the workbook provides you a written road map of your healing. Second, you can join a virtual support group to discuss your personal struggles with your toxic mother, where you can encourage or be encouraged by the real-life stories of sons from all walks of life. Third, you may wish to create your own fellowship group of men you would like to encourage or whom you would like to encourage you. My website invites you to plan a retreat with your personal set of friends or "family" to help you all work toward developing a unified, healing, and safe community in which to love and be loved boldly. Fourth, you can be

inspired by real-life stories of men who are taking charge of their own healing. Or, you can share your own. We sons must remove the stigma of showing how we have successfully created a healthy path of healing for our-selves and each other. You can find that kind of encour-agement on my website too.

We sons of toxic mothers need not read self-help books in a vacuum, but neither do we need to shy from them. Remember, one of the three principles of walking into your world equipped to heal and love boldly is to seek the healthy input of others. One way to do this is to seek input from professionals such as therapists, counselors, and doctors. Another is to read expert advice from professionals. And, still another is to read self-help books and others written by authors with firsthand knowledge of and experience with issues similar to yours. The key is to start the journey with humility and honesty as you inventory your life and assess the quality of your relationships. Challenge your comfort levels. Prepare for a fight but hope for the best with all your heart. Envision yourself a man of integrity and character, practicing virtues you have not even considered possible and performing acts of love, grace, and mercy without the personal, toxic demand that someone return the favor. Imagine yourself with the confidence to love others boldly with the wisdom of knowing how you need to be loved just the same. Set yourself on a path to walk in the freedom that you do not need the approval of your toxic mother, but you are healing enough to move in or out of a rela-tionship with her without compromising your dignity. By definition, you are her son! By Grace and your hard work of healing, you can become your own man!

ACKNOWLEDGMENTS

To God, Almighty, who has blessed me with the life I live, including the lessons that have helped me love Him and others better every day.

In June of 1981, Martin Jones, a man not much older than I, introduced himself to me in a way that immediately piqued my curiosity. He was confident, quirky, and, above all else, healthy! He was mentally healthy, showing me how men can think for themselves. He was emotionally healthy, never claiming to have all the right answers, but assured he knew Someone Who did. He loved me boldly. He restored to me a clear understanding of my own identity. He helped me understand who I am and Whose I am. His independence and maturity were unscathed, and he lived his life with freedom. Not freedom from a slave master, but a freedom to serve the One Who created freedom itself. He introduced me to that Someone Whose love had jettisoned him into the world: Jesus, Himself. And from that day forward, my choice to follow the Healer has placed me on a path to find healing from so much pain and grief.

If Jesus is the constant, Marie, my loving and amazing wife, is the exponent. In my deepest valleys and highest mountain tops, she has celebrated the life, love, and Grace we have had together for almost four decades. She never wavered when I wanted to quit my job as an academic. She has supported me as my life and career floundered from one thing to another. When I said I needed to find counseling, she was there. And, after experiencing my mother's abuses towards us both and after grieving with me over the loss of my entire family of origin, and after encouraging me as I grew to love her and others boldly, she supported my decision to help my mother during Mom's six-month terminal illness. And, Marie's support continued as I committed to putting these words together. I love you more!

To Marie's parents, Vic and Roddy Flow, I have written you a thousand times how much you taught your daughter to be loving, generous, smart, and adventurous. You did this by example. I never tire of your stories, and appreciate more than you know how much you welcomed me into your family.

To my daughter, Hope, here's my book. I anticipate yours even more than mine. My joy has always been to encourage you to speak your voice as loudly and skillfully as possible. To my son, Matthew, I marvel at how you remain so empathetic and kind with a father so full of . . . toxicity. Maybe one day you and I can write the sequel to this book together. You and your sister both know the art of forgiveness and have learned it better than I was ever able to teach you. This book is dedicated to you both. Thank you for your loving acceptance of me, a work in progress.

To Dave Verhaagen, I can only say thank you! Throughout our amazing and lengthy friendship, I have been in the infectious presence of your unfettered humor, your clear and compelling thinking, your professional work ethic, your gracious and graceful relational skills, your love and support for your wife, kids, and my family, and so, so much more. Your advice for writing this book came as a result of your encouragement for me to fearlessly define myself in the midst of my own gifts and baggage. As I read your prolific works, I become a better writer, but as I live life with you, I become a better husband, father, friend, and man. Thank you!

Yasser Youssef, who knew this book would happen after that one of so many walks when you challenged me take a risk and become a writer? Your friendship has blessed me over so much time. We have walked together literally and figuratively through grief, joy, confusion, fear, celebrations, boats, bikes, and blogging. You are my best friend. Your "path to lead" has always included loving me boldly, restoring me to a better relationship with myself and the gifts God has given me to love and serve others.

Geoffrey Berwind, the day you offered to work through this book with me was the day I experienced the blessings of someone putting into practice every principle included in it. Not since my former mentor has any man extended such a hand of Grace and love to me. Your skills at "hearing the edits needed" as I ramble aloud are only matched by your support and encouragement of me during the entire writing process. As humbled as I was, you simply continued to elevate me and my work until I could return to writing—that which brings me joy and healing and purpose and more! Thank you!

To Cristina Smith . . . Geoffrey and I loved the Star Trek-themed first version of this book! But you were the impetus behind convincing me to help others heal! For that I thank you. This book wrote itself after your input. Your title endured!

Debra Englander, any words I would use to thank you for your encouragement and support would fall short, especially on the ears of an editor of your magnitude! You kept me writing and you kept my spirits high, always helping me see the next step or a glimpse of hope. Thank you for showing me the power of words and writing.

To Jayne Lessard and my current therapist, only because you did not shy away or humiliate me in the midst of my pain can I believe there is hope for us all. With your help, I have healed enough to hear and listen to other men's pain and love them boldly. By the Grace of God, no story is too grotesque for the power of God to redeem. You live this every day for so many, and it inspires me to embrace the One who can work IN me and THROUGH me. I write with tears of gratitude and only hope to honor you and your work through this book.

Dan Allender, your book, Bold Love, inspired me to focus my healing and become a better man so many years ago. Who would have thought that 30 years later, you would encourage me to use your book's leading theme to focus my work? Your response to this project reflects the joy, love and support that can only come by being loved ever more boldly than we will love others. Thank you for believing in me.

Ralph Isaacson, these pages contain only a tiny fraction of what I shared with you—things so dark and so desolate, I believed no one could love someone as tattered and tormented as I. But you did! I hope this book, and your story in it, will inspire a whole generation of men to live out the transformational love of God and follow your example. I am forever grateful to have loved and been loved by a man willing to run the race to its completion. I'm still running, and I'll run until God says, "It is finished."

To my father in heaven, while you are not my heavenly Father, you have blessed me with gifts that only a father can give to his son. I have your sense of humor, and I smile with grief when I catch myself thinking I can no longer call you up and tell you a joke only you would appreciate. I also have your verbal gifts. While your circumstances brought you into the workplace after high school, your gift for words and language passed down to me like a constantly regenerating bank account. Just like you lived your life, sometimes the money wasn't there but the words were. And, when the words weren't there, you simply waited for the bank to compound the interest and discover a new word in the account. Your words never failed you even on the last day we spoke. I love you.

Mom, when the room went quiet and I realized you had stopped breathing, I ran to you and grabbed your hand. I was elated for you. My words said it all: "You made it! You're with Jesus!" And, just to reinforce that you still had one more rule-to-live-by, you took three more breaths and went to see the Lord. You and I discussed that your choice to die secretly left a burden on me—physically and emotionally. I was probably not going to be there in your last breath. You were OK with that, but you also acknowledged my sense of limitation and regret that it was only I who would be there for you. You said I didn't need to pressure myself to be there all the time. Like the tenderest of mothers, you gave me freedom to take care of myself during those last days. Standing 24/7 by your bedside waiting for you to die was an unrealistic goal. But, in the end, you gave me what I was secretly wishing—to be there for you in your last moment with your favorite Christian music playing loudly. Thank you for loving me. I am honored to be your son.

ANNOTATED ENDNOTES
BY CHAPTER

Introduction

1   BetterHelp Editorial Team Updated April 6, 2022) https://www.betterhelp.com/advice/teenagers/what-is-a-toxic-mother-and-how-does-she-affect-relationships

2   Kathy Hardie-Williams, (2016), and Adams, K. M. (2007)

3   See the following two researchers:

Lynch, Louise and Long, Maggie (2018). "Young Men, Help-Seeking, and Mental Health Services: Exploring Barriers and Solutions." *American Journal of Men's Health* 2018, Vol. 12(1) 138–149. Los Angeles, CA: Sage Publications, Inc.

McKenzie, Sarah K., Collings, Sunny, and Jenkins, Gabrielle (2018). "Masculinity, Social Connectedness, and Mental Health: Men's Diverse Patterns of Practice." *American Journal of Men's Health*, Vol. 12(5), 1247-1261. Los Angeles, CA: Sage Publications, Inc.

Chapter 2

4   There are many clinical and research sources that diagnose and treat dysfunction within a family. Most focus on specific symptoms or presentations. "Toxic" sometimes serves to clump many different psychological issues into one category. Consider the following article as an example: Nicole Letourneau, Lubna Anis, et. al. (2020). "Attachment and Child Health (ATTACH) pilot trials: Effect of parental reflective function intervention for families affected by toxic stress." *Infant Mental Health Journal*. Vol. 41(4), July-August 2020, 445-462.

5   Dwyer, Dale James (2019). "The Challenge of Indecision: Why do some people suffer from decidophobia?" *Psychology Today*. https://www.psychologtoday.com Posted April 25, 2019.

6   Elisabetta Franzoso, https://www.elisabettafranzoso.com

7   Rick Belden, December, 2017. https://www.huffpost.com/entry/men-and-the-mother-wound_b_9720718 Listen, too, to an interview with Rick Belden where he describes his work with men who suffer from Mother Wounds. https://www.youtube.com/watch?v=q4aL3WIWqZU His website, rickbelden.com was instrumental in my own healing. It helped me especially learn to reflect on what mattered. In addition, you can connect with his clear and guiding language and ideas by seeking points of interest in his website full of current content that helps men heal from their mother wound: https://www.menandthemotherwound.com

Chapter 3

8   Pearson, Catharine (2021). "5 Toxic Behaviors Parents Engage In – Without Realizing It." *HuffPost* 7-14-2021.

9   BetterHelp Editorial Team (2021) https://www.betterhelp.com/advice/teenagers/what-is-a-toxic-mother-and-how-does-she-affect-relationships/. BetterHelp is an amazing resource to help you determine if you should seek professional help and determine what kind of help you need.

10 I highly recommend Bryn Collins's book *The Toxic Parents Survival Guide: Recognizing, Understanding and Freeing Yourself from These Difficult Relationships* (Deerfield Beach, FL: Health Communications, Inc.): 2018.

11 Martin Kantor's book Passive-aggression: *A Guide for the Therapist, the Patient and the Victim* (Westport, CT: Praeger): 2002, is a very extensive study in passive-aggressive behavior and its effects on victims.

12 Consider anything written by Brené Brown and others like the following for more insight into setting healthy boundaries: Tawwab, Nedra Glover (2021). *Set Boundaries, Find Peace: A Guide to Reclaiming Yourself* (New York: TarcherPerigee).

13 DomesticShelters.org (November 11, 2015). What is Gaslighting?

Chapter 4

14 Information regarding mother wounds comes with an agenda. Most researchers, even in the purely medical field, focus on the more recent and militant feminist perspective of men and masculinity. It is up to you to sift through the politics and bias to discover what exactly you wish to heal. Even the idea of "mother wound" leaves the door open for you to play the victim role instead of taking full responsibility for your life, growth, and healing. See Chapter 8, "Heal What Matters" to begin focusing your goals and objectives in healing your personal wound.

15 See books like Bryn Collins's book mentioned above, Nick Nolan's book *No Place Like Home: Coping with the Decline and Death of Toxic Parents* (Los Angeles: Little Eden Press): 2019, or Lindsay C. Gibson's book *Recovering from Emotionally Immature Parents: Practical Tools to Establish Boundaries and Reclaim Your Emotional Autonomy* (Oakland: New Harbinger Publications, Inc.): 2019.

Chapter 5

16 Tony Fahkry (2018). "Even Though Your Wounds Are Not Your fault, Your Healing Is Still Your Responsibility." https://medium.com/the-mission/even-though-your-wounds-are-not-your-fault-your-healing-is-still-your-responsibility-d17d86f228d8

17 Although a bit outdated, Alice Miller's book, *For Your Own Good* (New York: Farrar, Straus, Giroux): 1990, was a hallmark book that shaped my understanding of punishment and opened up the floodgates to examine how my mother's punishments were simply cruel attempts at capturing control and power.

18 See Karen Young's blog, Hey Sigmund, here: https://www.heysigmund.com/?s=karen+young

19 Karen Young

20 Brianna Wiest and January Nelson. https://thoughtcatalog.com/january-nelson/2019/10/what-happened-to-you-was-not-your-fault-but-how-you-go-forward-is-your-responsibility/

21 Many in the psychology field call this "self-care." This book presents many different perspectives of self-care tips. For one perspective on self-care for adult children, see *Coping with Critical, Demanding, and Dysfunctional Parents: Powerful Strategies to Help Adult Children Maintain Boundaries and Stay Sane* (Oakland: New Harbinger

Publications, Inc.): 2018, by David M. Allen. There are many other approaches from which to choose. Find the one that works best for you.

Chapter 6

22 I highly recommend J.D. Vance's book, *Hillbilly Elegy* (New York: Harper): 2018. It not only portrays my mother's and my upbringing in stark detail, but it represents another perspective of how "sins of the fathers" are passed on to the next generation.

23 Some mental health professionals simply call this "self-talk." There are many types of self-talk such as motivational, silent, and educational. The research looks at how we can increase positive self-talk and decrease negative. In addition, the researchers investigate the effects of positive and negative varieties of self-talk on performance such as academic or athletic. See sources like:

Tod, David & Hardy, James & Oliver, Emily. (2011). "Effects of Self-Talk: A Systematic Review." *Journal of Sport & Exercise Psychology* 33, 666-87. 10.1123/jsep.33.5.666.

Oliver, Joe and Bennett, Richard. (2020). *The Mindfulness and Acceptance Workbook for Self-Esteem: Using Acceptance & Commitment Therapy to Move Beyond Negative Self-Talk & Embrace Self-Compassion* (Oakland: Harbinger Publications, Inc).

Chapter 7

24 Jackson MacKenzie, in his book *Psychopath Free* (New York: Berkley Books): 2015, explains this same pattern with an accompanying "tight feeling in [his] heart." But his NEXT book, *Whole Again* (New York: TarcherPerigee): 2019, explains very well how to climb out of the negative cycles and toward becoming "whole again" or healed. I recommend both.

25 Aly McCarthy, March, 2018, Families of Character, "What Are the 40 Virtues: Full List." https://www.familiesofcharacter.com/blogs/family/what-are-the-40-virtues-full-list

26 McCarthy, Aly (March, 2018) https://www.familiesofcharacter.com/blogs/family/what-are-the-40-virtues-full-list

27 The list of virtues is taken partially from the following websites:

https://www.virtuesforlife.com/what-are-virtues/

https://en.wikipedia.org/wiki/Virtue

https://bit.ly/37SVRLi

Chapter 8

28 Here, it must be noted that the absence of joy and seeking healthy pleasure such as fun and social interactions is quite related to depression. First, if your healing journey does not bring you to a place where you can define and pursue joy and fun, you are encouraged to seek counseling from a professional. Second, one extreme reaction to toxic mothers is to become hedonistic. This is not the same as joy. Learn the difference from a professional.

29 Many therapists and self-help books advise people who come from dysfunctional families to construct a true family for themselves. It might consist of a relative, close friends, and a therapist. This family will help provide you the safety, support, and love you need to continue moving into your world with your new RTLB.

30 Many men become addicted to any number of things due to their extreme escape away from their toxic situation with their mothers. Recovery groups serve a great purpose as do intensive therapy groups such as https://www.trueface.org that provide you with intensive, confidential therapy one-on-one or in groups. I highly recommend them.

31 https://www.merriam-webster.com/dictionary/integrity

32 Adapted from New International Version

Chapter 9

33 For more information on mature parenting, consider these references as a starting point:

Peg Streep, "What Makes a Good Mother Anyway?" (October 2013). https://www.psychologytoday.com/us/blog/tech-support/201310/what-makes-good-mother-anyway

Meeker, Meg (2015). *Strong Mothers, Strong Sons: Lessons Mothers Need to Raise Extraordinary Men.* (New York: Ballantine Books).

34 Self-protection is a root of lots of dysfunction within relationships. For more information on self-protection, its effects on the human psyche and ways to address it, consider beginning with these references:

Larrick, R. (1993). "Motivational factors in decision theories: the role of self-protection." *Psychological Bulletin.*

Alicke, M., & Sedikides, C. (2009). "Self-enhancement and self-protection: What they are and what they do." European Review of Social Psychology 20, 1-48.

35 Allendar, Dan and Longman, Tremper (1992). *Bold Love.* (Colorado Springs: Nav Press).

36 According to Julie Smith, an educator, spiritual director and a Certified Narrative Enneagram Teacher, "The Enneagram is a tool for individual and collective transformation. Gaining insight into our own patterns allows freedom to choose our responses. The enneagram awakens compassion for ourselves and fellow human beings as we journey through life."

37 *StrengthsFinders 2.0* (New York: Gallup Press): 2007, by Tom Rath, is the best and quickest way to begin to understand how you take in the world. After taking the online assessment (which is quite fun), you are provided a list of the five top strengths with an explanation of so many applications to the real world: job selection, skills, and talents that lend themselves best to those strengths, advantages, and benefits of having such strengths and more.

38 There is an entire body of psychological research on happiness. It defines happiness and identifies proactive things we can do to build happiness into our lives. The key here is to believe that you deserve to be happy, something many men with toxic mothers tend to doubt. Consider consulting academic and non-academic sources like these:

Myers, David G. and Diener, Ed. "The Pursuit of Happiness: New Research Uncovers Some Anti-Intuitive Insights Into How Many People Are Happy—And Why." *Scientific American*, Vol. 274(5), May 1996, 70-72.

Napawan, Anna (2021) *Happiness Workbook: A CBT-Based Guide to Foster Positivity and Embrace Joy.* (Emeryville, CA: Rockridge Press).

39 Wonderful work is being done regarding "mindset." Consider this original source to provide you some more detail and direction.

Dweck, Carol S. (2007). *Mindset: The New Psychology of Success.* (New York: Ballantine Books).

Chapter 10

40 I recommend *The One-Minute Apology* by Ken Blanchard and Margret McBride (New York: William Morrow): 2003.

41 https://hr.nih.gov/sites/default/files/public/documents/working-nih/mentoring/pdf/tips-mentees.pdf

42 https://www.franchisegrowthpartners.com/?s=good+mentor. An interesting note. Most of the books on mentoring for youngsters who struggle with toxic mothers are directed specifically at women. This book can encourage you to think creatively if you want to begin mentoring young men on the same issue. Using this RTLB approach to healing, as sons, we can adapt the content in books both for generic mentoring and for mentoring women in unhealthy relationships with their mothers.

Chapter 11

43 The effects of toxic shame run quite deep in the soul of a son. Here are two sources that address the idea of shame, humiliation, and humility. Humility, of course is the virtue we can integrate into our RTLB. Humiliation must be detected, whether we receive it from our mothers or we, ourselves, humiliate others.

Wright, Alan D. (2010). *Free Yourself, Be Yourself: Find the Power to Escape Your Past*. (Colorado Springs: Multnomah Books). Previously published under the title *Shame Off You*.

Bradshaw, John (2010). *Healing the Shame that Binds You*. Kindle Edition. (Deerfield Beach, FL: Health Communications, Inc.).

44 Researchers, especially Yousaf and Hunter, have pointed out the unique way men approach their need for professional help. It appears that "masculinity" clouds our judgment as men. The following are two articles that describe the obstacles to sons taking the first step toward healing. My advice is reductionist. Until you feel stuck and want to get unstuck, you will probably stay in your toxic environment and be manipulated by your mother's RTLB.

Yousaf, O., Grunfeld, E.A. and Hunter, M.S. (2015) "A systematic review of the factors associated with delays in medical and psychological help-seeking among men." *Health Psychology Review* 9 (2), 264-276. http://dx.doi.org/10.1080/17437199.2013.840954

Yousaf, O., Popat, A., & Hunter, M. S. (2015). "An investigation of masculinity attitudes, gender, and attitudes toward psychological help-seeking." *Psychology of Men & Masculinity* 16(2), 234-237. https://doi.org/10.1037/a0036241

45 While there is much hope for group therapy to benefit sons of toxic mothers, there are many obstacles too. Privacy, shame, trauma, and confidentiality many times detract from the ability to form effective therapy groups. This is an even stronger case for why we as sons must take responsibility for our own healing and find whatever works. This book attempts to put the options into an understandable framework.

46 If you are curious about Cognitive Behavioral Therapy, there are many sources that describe it in detail, such as this textbook: Craske, Michelle G. (2010). *Theories of psychotherapy. Cognitive–behavioral therapy.* (Washington, DC: American Psychological Association).

47 There are so many books that can help you gain insight into your strengths and weaknesses, discover your purpose and design your mission, all while teaching you the value of working in a profession and job. I suggest the following. They are clearly written and provide you many different avenues to explore the concepts they present.

The Purpose-Driven Life (Grand Rapids, MI: Zondervan): 2013, by Rick Warren, provides reflection exercises to help you learn what drives you. Whether you agree with the Christian perspective, Warren helps you contemplate the universals of why we are here and how we search for meaning. The book allows you to connect with those purposes.

Your Work Matters to God (Colorado Springs: Nav Press): 1990, by Doug Sherman and William Hendricks, provides a platform to examine your work life and the underlying assumptions out of which you execute your calling. It is both sobering and inspiring.

StrengthsFinders 2.0 (New York: Gallup Press): 2007, by Tom Rath, is the best and quickest way to begin to understand how you take in the world. After taking the online assessment (which is quite fun), you are provided a list of the five top strengths with an explanation of so many applications to the real world: job selection, skills, and talents that lend themselves best to those strengths, advantages, and benefits of having such strengths and more.

GUY ARCURI

AUTHOR, SPEAKER, MEDIA CONTRIBUTOR

Since 1981, Guy Arcuri has enjoyed life as a University academic and "teacher of all things." With a Ph.D. from UNC-Chapel Hill in Curriculum and Instruction, he still generates revenue coaching teachers and school administrators, writing and editing curriculum guides for corporations and other organizations, leading men's retreats, and teaching Spanish to students young and old. In the most recent years, he has gratefully and successfully morphed himself into a writer, and this is his first book.

In all of his endeavors, one universal theme continues to surface. People teach and learn best if they are able to reflect on how, but many do not have the skill-set or the time to reflect well. He dedicates his life to improving the lives of his clients by helping them reflect on their life, their choices and their impact on themselves and others in contexts ranging from personal to academic to professional. Learning to reflect on how one personally processes the world revolutionizes that person's ability to learn, grow, and succeed.

Arcuri has realized his adult successes and dreams *in spite of* the tragedy and pain he has overcome in his mother's world… what this book calls Hazel World. With Arcuri's youth limited by the mental illnesses and dysfunction of those around him including suffering from his mother's verbal, emotional and physical abuse, the heartbreak of losing his entire family of origin within nine years (sister, father, mother, brother) in combination with his deep commitment to Truth, Grace and Love, Arcuri believes it is his calling to help others, especially adult men who were or are being traumatized by their toxic mother, helping them heal and enjoy a life of respect, dignity, love, compassion or whatever other virtuous character trait they wish to express in and for themselves.

Married for almost four decades, he enjoys a healthy family life with his wife and two children in North Carolina. Volunteering to enter his mother's world to care for her during her terminal illness, despite the resentment he had for her, opened his eyes to the fact that he was about to conjure all he believed about life, love, anger and bitterness. Practicing what he preaches in this book until even his remaining brother left this world a month after his mother not only kept him sane, but led to his writing this book.

Made in United States
Troutdale, OR
04/05/2025

30343189R00115